Katherine Anne Porter's
POETRY

Katherine Anne Porter's
POETRY

Edited with an introduction by
Darlene Harbour Unrue

UNIVERSITY OF SOUTH CAROLINA PRESS

© 1996 University of South Carolina

Published in Columbia, South Carolina, by the
University of South Carolina Press

Manufactured in the United States of America

00 99 98 97 96   5 4 3 2 1

Library of Congress Cataloging-in-Publication Data

Porter, Katherine Anne, 1890–1980.
  Katherine Anne Porter's poetry / edited with an introduction
by Darlene Harbour Unrue
    p.   cm.
  Includes bibliographical references and index.
  ISBN 1–57003–084–7
  I. Unrue, Darlene Harbour. II. Title.
PS3431.O752A17   1996
811'.52—dc20   95–32494

For My Family:
Hazel, John,
Greg, Jane,
Shizuko, Kevin,
John Earl, and Virginia

Come, let us make a fair exchange
Of trivial sorrows for which men may die.
You would cry
For a false rhyme, and I
For a dead dragon-fly.

Come whisper lightly all your strange
And tenuous griefs and I in faith will tell you mine.

Katherine Anne Porter,
undated fragment, ca. 1923

Contents

Contents

Illustrations

Preface

I began gathering and editing Katherine Anne Porter's poetry several years ago when I became convinced that to ignore Porter's poetry was to ignore an important aspect of her art. My conviction of that importance strengthened with my increasing awareness of the relationship between Porter's poetry and her fiction and the firm rootedness of her poetry in the most deeply felt core of her personal experience. Analyzing Porter's poetry for its techniques and themes also supported my long-held contention that despite some critics' reluctance to place her in a movement, she was a modernist in the truest sense.

In the course of preparing this book I have become indebted to many people. Barbara Thompson Davis, literary trustee of the Katherine Anne Porter estate, gave support and permission to publish Porter's work and to reproduce photographs in the Porter collection at the University of Maryland. Paul Porter, Katherine Anne Porter's nephew, has been unstinting in his willingness to share time and memories with me. David Locher, Porter's student at the University of Michigan and a poet in his own right, contributed valuable information about Porter as a teacher of poetry. Deborah Wescott Clark, Barbara Harrison's daughter, supported my plan to reprint Katherine Anne Porter's *French Song-Book*, originally published by her mother, Barbara Harrison, and Monroe Wheeler. Matthew J. Bruccoli directed me to rare copies of the *French Song-Book* and a Porter poem in manuscript. Patricia Willis, curator of American literature at the Beinecke Rare Book and Manuscript Library at Yale University, and Cathy Henderson of the Harry Ransom Humanities Research Center at the University of Texas were efficiently responsive to my requests. My daughter, Jane, in New York and Mary Dengler at the University of Nevada were helpful researchers, and Charleen Gagliardi contributed her artist's insights to the poetry. I wish to thank especially Ruth M. Alvarez, curator of literary manuscripts in the Archives and Manuscripts Department of the University of Maryland at College Park Libraries, for invaluable help. The University of Nevada, Las Vegas, provided various kinds of institutional support. I am particularly grateful to former president Robert C. Maxson. I also thank English Department Chair Joseph B. McCullough. The help and support of my husband, John, have been as measureless as always.

In reprinting Porter's published poems I followed the printed text of their last appearance in print during her lifetime. The unpublished poems were found in various files in the Katherine Anne Porter Papers at the McKeldin Library at the University of Maryland at College Park, in various collections at the Beinecke Rare Book and Manuscript Library of Yale University, and in the Genevieve Taggard Papers at the New York Public Library. In selecting the texts for the unpublished poems, I chose what appeared to be the last version Porter produced. I have arranged the poems chronologically according to what I have determined to be the dates of their first drafts, occasionally in the face of conflicting dates Porter placed on different copies of a given poem. The differing degree of completeness of dates among the poems reflects Porter's inconsistent dating of them. Significantly different earlier versions of both published and unpublished poems are included in the appendix. Whenever possible I have preserved Porter's original, and sometimes peculiar, punctuation and spelling. Exceptions are her erratic use of periods that may look like ellipses. I have standardized such use by her to five. Any use of three in this book thus indicates an ellipsis. I also have altered the punctuation in the *French Song-Book* to conform to modern American usage by changing the single quotation marks of the original, indicating direct quotation, to double quotation marks. Rather than distinguishing among Porter's short stories, long stories, and short novels, I have placed in quotation marks the titles of all her fictional pieces except her long novel, *Ship of Fools.*

Grateful acknowledgement for permission to publish is made to the following:

Barbara Thompson Davis, trustee for the literay estate of Katherine Anne Porter, for permission to publish or quote from previously unpublished work by Katherine Anne Porter, to reprint previously published poems, and to reproduce phototgraphs in the Katherine Anne Porter Papers at the University of Maryland at College Park;

the University of College Park Libraries for permission to reprint and quote from unpublished material in the Katherine Anne Porter Papers, the Paul Porter Papers, and the Delafield Day Spier Papers and for permission to reproduce photographs from the Katherine Anne Porter Papers. References in the notes to McKeldin identify the library at the University of Maryland at College Park that houses the Special Collections;

Houghton Mifflin Co./Seymour Lawrence for permission to reprint the nine poems by Katherine Anne Porter included in *The Collected Essays and Occasional Writings of Katherine Anne Porter* (1970);

the *New York Herald Tribune,* Inc., for permission to reprint "Winter Burial," originally published in the *New York Herald Tribune Books;*

Grove/Atlantic, Inc., for permission to quote from *Letters of Katherine Anne Porter,* edited by Isabel Bayley (1990);

the New York Public Library, Rare Books and Manuscript Division, for permission to quote from letters in the Genevieve Taggard Papers;

Yale Collection of American Literature, the Beinecke Rare Book and Manuscript Library, Yale University, for permission to quote from material in the Josephine Herbst, Matthew Josephson, Russell Lynes, Ezra Pound, and Robert Penn Warren collections in the Yale Collection of American Literature.

Katherine Anne Porter's
POETRY

Introduction

During her apprenticeship Katherine Anne Porter experi-
mented with various kinds of artistic expression. She danced
and sang and acted, she wrote ballet librettos, she wrote fic-
tion, and she wrote poetry. By the end of 1924 she acknowl-
edged her métier—prose fiction—but she was never able to
abandon poetry completely. During her lifetime she published
only eleven original poems and twenty-one translations, but
she wrote several hundred more, most of which she destroyed
or lost.[1] Porter's unpublished poems that have survived, in frag-
mentary notes or in letters to friends or relatives, join her pub-
lished poems to create a unique commentary on her life and
works. Each of the poems is an index to a stage of her develop-
ing intellectual views or to a temporary emotional state, and
each poem also represents at a given time her cumulative expe-
rience and evolving literary background. Her translations, while
not tied directly to her personal experience, link her clearly to
the modernist tradition.

Porter's early poems bear the marks of older forms: ballad
metrics of hymns she had sung in the Methodist Church, En-
glish and American folk ballads she had performed on the Ly-
ceum circuit in 1914 in Texas and Louisiana, Renaissance and
Romantic lyric poetry to which her father introduced her, and
sonnets of Shakespeare she had memorized by the time she
was fifteen.[2] In the 1920s Porter layered onto her knowledge

1

of traditional English and American poetry an appreciation for the primitive poetry of Latin American poets and Mexican folk songs. Throughout the 1920s and 1930s while she nurtured a devotion to a broad range of late medieval literature, she also was drawn firmly into the modernist aesthetics of Yeats, Pound, and Eliot and from there expanded her poetic appreciation to include the works of, among others, Hart Crane, John Crowe Ransom, Robert Penn Warren, Allen Tate, W. H. Auden, Wallace Stevens, Archibald MacLeish, Marianne Moore, and William Carlos Williams. During these years she also read Baudelaire and Rimbaud in their original French, and Rilke in German.

Porter's poetry in some instances represents an early or intermediate phase in her creative process, which began with vaguely formed mental images and culminated in fiction,[3] the fiction paradoxically more dense and tightly woven than the poetry. Never a first-rate poet, by her own admission, Porter left behind a poetic canon that contains pleasant, original lyrics with occasionally memorable images or phrases, and translations that show her sensitivity to poetic sentiment expressed in languages she spoke and read at only an unsophisticated level. Some of Porter's poetry does have intrinsic merit, but the primary value of all her poems is that they are emblems for the crucial experiences of her life and for the subjects, forms, themes, images, and symbols of her more exquisitely wrought fiction.

Katherine Anne Porter was born Callie Russell Porter 15 May 1890, in Indian Creek, Texas, the fourth of five children of Harrison Boone Porter and Mary Alice Jones Porter, who died when Callie was two years old.[4] Callie's rearing was shared by her father and her paternal grandmother, Catharine Ann Skaggs Porter, the source of family legend carried from Kentucky and the model for the grandmothers in Porter's stories "The Downward Path to Wisdom" and "The Jilting of Granny

Weatherall" and in her short novel "The Old Order."[5] Porter's erratic formal education concluded abruptly after a year at the Thomas School in San Antonio when she was fifteen. A year later she married John Henry Koontz, whose family introduced her into the Roman Catholicism that would contribute to the religious and political themes of her poetry as well as her fiction. When Porter's marriage to Koontz ended nine years later, she legally changed her name to Katherine Anne Porter, a version of the name of the grandmother who had reared her. She also had begun the preparation for her writing career, which would span the greater part of the twentieth century.

Porter's flight from her first marriage and Texas in 1914 set her on a nomadic course that led through Illinois, Colorado, New York, Pennsylvania, Connecticut, Mexico, Bermuda, Louisiana, California, Michigan, and Europe, with only occasional sojourns in Texas. The years between 1914 and 1920 were marked by serious illnesses (tuberculosis in 1915–1917 and a nearly fatal influenza in 1918), possibly a second marriage, and apprentice writing. In New York in 1919 she met many bohemian writers and intellectuals who directed her to social and aesthetic ideas more revolutionary than those she already had. Among her New York acquaintances were Mexican artists who encouraged her to accept a magazine assignment that enabled her to go to Mexico in 1920. The Mexico period, a total of about three years between 1920 and 1931, was important to Porter because it provided the experiences upon which she based her first original pieces of fiction and some of her early poetry.[6]

When Porter left Mexico in 1931 for Europe, she was entering another phase of her traveling and writing that would solidify many of her political and aesthetic views. Before the Second World War was over, she had tried and rejected marriage two more times, first to Eugene Pressly from 1933 to 1938, and then to Albert Erskine from 1938 to 1942. In 1944 she replaced John Peale Bishop as a fellow at the Library of Congress.[7] Afterward she divided her time between New York and California, where for brief times she worked as a film studio scriptwriter. When she began to accept university appointments in 1947, she was struggling to finish her major work, a long novel begun in the late 1920s.[8] The struggle would last more than a dozen years before the work would appear as *Ship of Fools.*

After the publication of *Ship of Fools,* Porter traveled in Europe for a year and then returned to the United States, settling in the Washington, D.C., area. She spent the remainder of her life giving occasional readings and working sporadically on unfinished pieces from her past. She died in Silver Spring, Maryland, 19 September 1980. According to her request, her ashes were buried beside the grave of her mother in the family plot near Indian Creek.

At the end of 1922 Porter's first published story, "María Concepción," appeared in *Century* magazine. Up to that time, in addition to a large body of journalistic pieces, she had published one poem, four retellings of fables, a ghostwritten account of a young American woman's marriage to a Chinese student, and a pamphlet to accompany a Mexican folk-art exhibit to the United States.[9] "María Concepción" was among Porter's stories gathered in 1930 under the title *Flowering Judas*—a collection which included "Magic," "Rope," "He," and "The Jilting of Granny Weatherall" in addition to the title story. With the exception of "Theft," "The Martyr" and "Virgin Violeta," the slim volume represented the cumulative body of Porter's fiction at that point in her career.

Flowering Judas won immediate and enthusiastic praise from critics. In the *New Republic* Louise Bogan declared that there was "nothing quite like" Porter's talent, "very little" that approached "its strength in contemporary writing." Yvor Winters, writing in the *Hound & Horn,* said, "I can think of no living American who has written short stories at once so fine in detail, so powerful as units, and so mature and intelligent in outlook, except W. C. Williams." The critical success of the first edition of *Flowering Judas* fixed Porter's high position in American letters at the same time it earned her a Guggenheim Fellowship. When the collection was expanded in 1935 to include "Theft," "That Tree," "The Cracked Looking-Glass," and "Hacienda," the praise continued. John Chamberlain wrote in the *New York Times,* "After five years, the intensity of these stories seems just as important as it did when they were originally published."

By the time the first substantial critical article on Porter's work, Lodwick Hartley's "Katherine Anne Porter," appeared in the *Sewanee Review* in 1940, Porter had developed the Miranda cycle, and her second collection of fiction, *Pale Horse, Pale Rider: Three Short Novels,* had already made its appearance to an enthusiastic critical reception. Lewis Gannett called Porter one of the greatest American writers, and Paul Rosenfeld said that she moved in the illustrious company headed by Hawthorne, Flaubert, and Henry James. In spite of this critical praise, however, Porter's readership remained exclusive and relatively small, and throughout the 1930s, 1940s, and 1950s a disparity existed between the critical adulation of her work and the tentative appreciation of it by a popular audience. Robert Penn Warren began his 1942 essay on Porter, the now-classic "Irony with a Center," with a direct acknowledgement of the phenomenon. Porter's fiction, Warren claimed, had not found the public which its merit warranted. He traced the cause to Porter's refusal to compromise her artistic integrity for the popular market and to reviewers who in summarizing her work with phrases like "beautiful style" had unwittingly implied to potential readers that "exquisiteness" was substituted for substance and that the form of Porter's fiction was more noteworthy than the artistic vision the form conveyed. The disparity continued with the publication in 1952 of a collection of Porter's essays (*The Days Before*). Reviewers expanded their praise to include Porter's critical perception, but relatively few copies of her works were sold on the popular market. Already the recipient of two Guggenheim Fellowships, Porter began to receive other awards and appointments and to collect numerous honorary degrees.

After 1940 articles on Porter's work appeared at regular intervals. In 1957, the first book on Porter, *The Fiction and Criticism of Katherine Anne Porter,* by Harry John Mooney, Jr., was published. But not until the publication of *Ship of Fools* in 1962 did Porter's popular appeal catch up with her firmly established critical reputation and bring with it long-awaited financial reward. Her popularity on both fronts intensified with the publication of *The Collected Stories of Katherine Anne Porter,* which in 1966 won both the Pulitzer Prize and the National Book Award. She also was presented the Gold Medal for Fiction by the National Institute of Arts and Letters.[10] Her last works published during her lifetime were *The Collected Essays and Occasional Writings of Katherine Anne Porter* (1970), which included nine of her previously published poems, and *The Never-Ending Wrong* (1977), an autobiographical account of her participation in the Sacco-Vanzetti protest of 1927. Critics were more generous in their praise of the collection than they were of her fictionalized memoir, but no one singled out the poetry for commendation.

If suffering and uncertainty constituted the first thirty years of Katherine Anne Porter's life, these years represented as well the struggle of a female artist growing up in the rural and border South to find a vehicle of expression for her artistic energy and to break out of the restrictiveness of convention. From all accounts, the young Callie Porter was drawn to the arts and was most fulfilled when she was indulging her creativity. She loved to dance and sing and yearned to play a musical instrument. She recalled writing a child's version of a novel when she was about six years old and, with her childhood friend Erna Schlemmer, enacting the martyrdom of Joan of Arc with herself playing the tragic Joan.[11]

The formal education Porter received in country schools and by tutors brought in as boarders by her grandmother was not progressive but rather was grounded in an older literature. Porter said that from the age of twelve to twenty, her favorite writers were Dante, Shakespeare, Milton, Emily Brontë, Montaigne, Rabelais, Chekhov, and Henry James. She later added Voltaire, Jane Austen, and Keats, and she specifically identified Bishop Percy's *Reliques* and the ballads collected by Francis Child as works with which she was happily familiar. She nostalgically recalled going to vaudeville shows with her father and hearing old Negro folk songs, to which she always was drawn for their pure poetic sentiment.[12]

Out of this background came Porter's poem "Texas: By the Gulf of Mexico," written when she was twenty-two years old and still married to J. H. Koontz. With its awkward rhythm and rhymes and self-conscious Elizabethan language, "Texas: By the Gulf of Mexico" has little to recommend it for artistic merit. But it does reveal Porter's sensitivity to audience as she appeals to business men to come to Texas to make money. Her preference for a warm climate over "the frozen North" is sincerely conveyed in the images of "sunkissed fruits and flowers" and "fluttering jessamine trees," images she would associate all her life with an ideal "home." The poem also anticipates four of her later poems, "Now No Spring," "November in Windham," "Bouquet for October," and "After a Long Journey," in which she condenses a warm climate to a warm season and identifies it with both spiritual love and the artistic spirit.

When Porter left Koontz in 1914 and went to Chicago to find work, she earned a kind of living with small parts in movies. However, she soon returned to Texas to help her pregnant sister, Gay, whose husband had abandoned her. In Porter's struggle to support herself and to help Gay, she set out on the Lyceum circuit, relying on area ministers to secure engagements for her.[13] She put to use the dramatic skills she naturally had and some she had acquired in Chicago and San Antonio, and she performed the ballads she had learned from Percy and Child.

Porter's struggle to survive during 1914–1915 led to a physical breakdown, and in 1915–1917 she spent long months in Texas tuberculosis hospitals. Little was known about any writing or composing she might have done during this period, until the daughter of a woman who had been a fellow patient with Porter in the Carlsbad, Texas, tuberculosis sanitorium in 1916 sent Joan Givner (whose biography of Porter had appeared in 1982) several pages of a scrapbook that contained photographs of Porter as well as songs and poems written and coauthored by her. Several lyrics in Porter's handwriting compare the tedious medical rituals of the clinic with the dry Texas landscape ("it's a country of Hell-fire things"), Porter identifying this terrible period of her life with a place devoid of such growing things as the symbolic fruits and flowers and jessamine trees.[14]

Porter probably continued to write poetry during the next few years, but little is extant. Among her papers at the University of Maryland is a draft of an untitled two-stanza poem that begins "I choose beads." The poem rests on a series of images, visual and auditory, that evokes a primitive place represented in the poem by Samoa. The narrator claims a preference for beads, a drum, "a diminutive / Persistently tintinabulent / Tambourine," "an apron of redolent grasses," and "a wreath of irritable red flowers." Porter apparently included the poem in an unpreserved letter to a lover. She signed the poem and the letter "Katana, Queen of Samoan Dancers" and dated it "New York 1920, 17 Grove Street." Unfinished and unpolished, it reveals Porter's skill in creating effective images.

The only other poem by Porter thought to have survived from the first three decades of her life is "A Dying Child," written after the death of her six-year-old niece, Mary Alice Holloway, whom Porter also commemorated in the memoir "A Christmas Story" (1946). Porter, who was living in Denver when Mary Alice died, said she had an intuition of the death at the moment it occurred. She was always to say that this death pained her more than any other.[15] By the time Porter wrote "A Dying Child" in 1920, she had had substantial journalistic experience writing columns and reviewing vaudeville shows and plays, experience that honed her style and sharpened her point of view. She also had continued to read and to broaden her literary background. It is nevertheless her familiarity with the ballad and her fondness for the lyric that surface most strongly and work together in this poem.

The poem probably was written in the autumn of 1920, either before Porter left New York or shortly after she first arrived in Mexico. Each time Porter recopied it in later years, she revised it. The first version appeared untitled in a letter to her family, the poem sent specifically to Gay, Mary Alice's mother (see Appendix).[16] In the eight years since "Texas: By the Gulf of Mexico," Porter had moved to a straight-forward, pure language, abandoning self-consciously archaic diction once and for all. The grief that was the source of the poem allowed no artificiality and marked a point when pure feeling and pure language came together for Porter.

"A Dying Child" is a lyrical lamentation which does not progress to consolation and thus is not an elegy in the truest sense. Relying on incremental repetition and alternating end rhymes in each of the two roughly metered quatrains (standard features of the ballad), Porter repeats the last two lines of the first quatrain in reverse order as the last two lines of the second quatrain, offering a slight linguistic variation on the central phrase, "Oh, dearly, dearly [do] I love the light of day," and an alternative image for "the growing things that flower or run" ("the dress the summer garden wears"). When Porter recopied this poem in 1953 for her cousin Gertrude Beitel, she revised it to apostrophize Mary Alice, and she eliminated the direct quotes and other marks of punctuation to make the lines more fluid.[17]

During Porter's three visits in Mexico between November 1920 and October 1923, her first original pieces of fiction and her first mature poems were written and published, most of them inspired by the heady experience of Mexico and the cultural revolution occurring there. Steeping herself in Mexico's history and current politics, Porter was at the same time trying to find her most comfortable artistic medium. Working occasionally as a journalist and writing essays on Mexican affairs, as well as writing fiction, she also was composing or translating poetry. The poetry she published in 1922 and afterwards, when she had hit her stride as a writer of fiction, shows an interesting amalgam of influences from her past readings and from modern writers, including some symbolist poets she had begun to read.

When Porter returned to New York from Mexico in the summer of 1922, she took a room with breakfast at 61 Washington Square South in Greenwich Village. Her head was still filled with thoughts of Mexico, and within a few months she completed "Two Ancient Mexican Pyramids—" for the *Christian Science Monitor* and, in a burst of feverish creativity, "María Concepción." During this period, Porter also wrote "Song with Castanet Accompaniment," which was never published. It can be dated by the Washington Square address typed on the left bottom corner of the surviving manuscript. Although it is a relatively short poem of only four quatrains, it is introduced by no fewer than three epigraphs drawn from poems by T. S. Eliot ("Whispers of Immortality"), Elinor Wylie ("Full Moon"), and A. E. Housman ("XLIII: The Immortal Part" in *A Shropshire Lad*). The subject of all four poems is death.

The initial six lines of "Song with Castanet Accompaniment" describe a "she" of the poem who sees reflected in a mirror her skeletal image—a use of an ancient superstition about mirrors and an anticipation of Porter's use of mirrors in her story "The Cracked Looking-Glass" (1932) and in her long novel, *Ship of Fools*. The last stanza poses a rhetorical question, "Who weaponed me with melting flesh / To war with potent rain and sun——[?]" The reference to the ravages of the sun on mortals is an allusion to Shakespeare's "Fear No More the Heat of the Sun," one of Porter's favorites among Shakespeare's lyrics.[18] The question addressing elemental issues also echoes Blake's "What immortal hand or eye / Could frame thy fearful symmetry?" and "Did he who made the Lamb make thee?"[19]

In spite of the allusion to Shakespeare and echoes of Blake, however, Porter acknowledges with the epigraphs the relevance of modern poems to her "Song." In the spirit of modern poetics, she delineates the irony of human destiny by juxtaposing the external and internal and by the naive human voice questioning the ways of fate. Porter reduces death to the frivolous ("I shall rattle like shaken dice") and the commonplace ("My ribs shall chatter like housewife's keys") with a macabre humor. The reader soon learns that the title's "Castanet Accompaniment" to the "Song" is the rattle of bones.

The first poem Porter published during the 1920s was "Enchanted," and in tone it reflects other kinds of pieces about Mexico she was writing during the same period.[20] "Enchanted" shows Porter's continuing reliance on the familiar ballad and lyric forms. The rhythm and rhyme are rigid with some strategic variation. The most arresting image in the poem is the "wraith of fiery magic" passing alliteratively "over my dark door sill." The "familiar stones" of the first line of the second stanza and the "tranquil roofs" of the first line of the second stanza are brought together in the last stanza as symbols of reality to be magically transformed should the roofs and the stones become "blooming roofs" and "singing stones." By implication it is the clear-visioned artist who has the ability to effect the transformation.

"Enchanted" shows the influence of Porter's Mexican experience, the actions of the first stanza a description of Porter's own movements as she routinely entered her house at 20 Calle Eliseo, within walking distance of downtown Mexico City. Years later Porter recalled vividly among her earliest impressions of Mexico narrow stone streets and the roof tops of houses locked together so that a person could walk from one roof to another.[21] Thematically the poem expresses Porter's enchantment with Mexico in the early 1920s and her initial idealistic faith in the Mexican cultural revolution. It is also a tribute to Mexico as a source of her artistic inspiration. Her exhortation and apostrophe to the "swift hunting moon," an allusion to Diana, echo the older lyrics she had loved in her youth. She pleads for a respite from the confusions of physical love so that she can luxuriate in the enchantment of the imaginary and the metaphysical, the realm of the artist. In the allusion to Diana she poses cupidity against an artistic ideal, a conflict she was to experience much of her life and was to treat in much of her short fiction.[22]

The influence of the Nicaraguan poet Salomón de la Selva is apparent in "Enchanted." De la Selva had come to Mexico in 1921, and Porter had a love affair with him either that same year or early in 1922. Their discussions of poetry and their reading it together, her inclusion in his circle of poet friends (among them, Carlos Pellicer, Jaime Torres Bodet, and José Gorostiza),[23] and Porter's appreciation of some of De la Selva's poems doubtless encouraged her own attempts at poetry. She particularly liked of De la Selva's poem "Birds of Clay," included in his collection *Tropical Town and Other Poems* (1918), copying the poem by hand, preserving it among her papers, and

admiring it long after she had developed a considerable con-
tempt for its author as a person. "Birds of Clay" is a three-
quatrain lyric in which the speaker compares little clay whistles
shaped like birds to his own skeletal remains and wishes the
vestige of his mortal existence could be the means by which
innocents would make art:

> When I am dead I want to lie
> Where in the centuries to be
> Children shall utter song and cry
> Through the wingèd dust of me.

The lyrical ballad form, which Porter had attempted in "A Dying
Child," would have appealed to her here. The subject of death
also interested her as she was developing her own variation on
the theme of death as a source of life.[24] Porter's image of the
wind blowing through her house is a version of De la Selva's
image of breath blowing through clay. Her prayer to Diana to
protect her from the seduction of romantic love may have been
related to her love affair with De la Selva.

When Porter arrived in Mexico in 1920, in addition to a
broad background of traditional poetry and an acquaintance-
ship with modern poetry, she brought with her an appreciation
for caricature and parody. In notes dated 1968 Porter recalled
seeing when she was ten or eleven years old a caricature of
Émile Zola. She said she learned a lesson "in that flash of a
glimpse of a comic drawing."[25] Her early reading of satirists
such as Rabelais and her youthful exposure to the drawings
and paintings of Dürer and Holbein fueled her appreciation,
but her fullest understanding of caricature with its attendant
modes of parody and satire occurred during her experiences in
Mexico, where caricature and satire had existed in refined forms
for many years.

In 1920 Porter met the young Miguel Covarrubias and other graphic caricaturists, and she encountered firsthand Mexico's lively tradition of parody and satire. The concepts of caricature that she blended into her own modernist ironic stance would continue throughout her life to influence both her fiction and her nonfiction. Her intellectual understanding of caricature is illustrated in her 1925 review of Covarrubias's collection of satirical portraits, *The Prince of Wales and Other Famous Americans.* In such satire, Porter saw a "deadly discernment of the comic in the other person," a pointing to a "defect or weakness, preferably an irremediable one, in the opponent." Porter considered indispensable to the caricaturist "the social gift of malice." At his or her best, like Covarrubias, the artist "in a few strokes" creates three dimensions and "something else that belongs to Metaphysics," "an inner quality" the subject has spent a lifetime "trying to hide, or disguise."[26] The review shows the degree to which Porter understood the primary intent of caricature, which contributed to her pure, clean style in both prose fiction and poetry and served her method of characterization in her fiction.

In the early 1920s Porter experimented with both caricature and parody. She wrote at least two parodies of De la Selva's poetry and one of a poem by Edna St. Vincent Millay. In the case of De la Selva, there is the expected element of malice, as in caricature—a clear intent on Porter's part to deflate and make comic De la Selva's pretentiousness and also his habit of preying on hapless females.[27] She later sent the following poem to Delafield Day:

> Lady trailing your gown
> Hiding your li-i-i-ttahl fee-eet
> Let me sing you a roun-de-laaaaaaaaay
> In the dust of the street!

Let me sell you a rhy-hime
For-or-or a bright penny!
Now is as good a ti-hiiime
To love, to love, to love, as GOOOOOOOOD
A time, to love as any!

Porter told Day that the song was a parody of De la Selva's "style, his rhyme scheme, and philosophy."[28] A more polished version of the song is the parody Porter called "Variation 1001: To the Foolish Virgins Who Aren't Gathering Roses." In 1957 she described it as her "parody of Salomón de la Selva's sentimental little poems" and dated it spring 1922.[29] In an allusion to Herrick, she takes double aim at De la Selva, forcing an unequal comparison between him and one of the Cavalier poets, whom she had long admired.

At about the same time, Porter wrote a parody of the first stanza of Edna St. Vincent Millay's "The Poet and His Book," which contains the line "Down, you mongrel, Death!" Porter begins her untitled poem "Down, you Mongrel Death." She said she wrote it soon after Millay's poem appeared, guessing 1922.[30] In the parody of Millay, Porter is stinging but less vitriolic than she is in her attacks on De la Selva. She never liked Millay or her poetry very much, considering Millay's verses too sentimentally feminine, but in a 1924 review Porter did pay tribute to Millay's *Distressing Dialogues*, a literary joke written under the pen name of Nancy Boyd. Porter declared that "Boyd" was Millay's "imp," the other half of a literary partnership, "Millay's lower nature." Porter praises the "low topical humor" of the book, which she says she loves because "there's not a kind line in it."[31]

Porter saw *Distressing Dialogues* as Millay's travesty of her refined sonnet-making self, and Porter approved of the satire. It was in fact the calculated nature of satire as well as caricature and parody that appealed to Porter, who regarded skill in such attack as an art. Hereafter Porter was not inclined to write poetic parodies, although she occasionally wrote little ditties that poked fun at one poet or another, such as the following:

> Of Mr. Sandburg's pomes I do
> So quickly get a crawful,
> For at his worst he's very bad,
> But at his best he's awful![32]

Porter's fiction is peopled with artists and others who indulge their malice in parody or caricature. Examples are Violeta ("Virgin Violeta"), Ramón ("The Martyr"), Carlos ("Hacienda"), Charles Upton ("The Leaning Tower"), and Jenny Brown (*Ship of Fools*).

In the late winter of 1922 and the early spring of 1923, when Porter was likely to have written her parody of Millay, she was living in New York but continuing to write about Mexico. She was recognized as an articulate authority on the political and cultural changes taking place in Mexico. Essays and book reviews by her were sought and readily published, and she was offered a chance to return to Mexico as the art editor of a planned Mexican issue for *Survey Graphic*. When Porter first returned to Mexico in late spring of 1923, she was thrown back into Mexican political events and confronted with reminders of her personal conflicts, intrigues, and love affairs of 1921 and 1922.

The years 1923 and 1924 marked Porter's greatest productivity as a poet and, ironically, also her first acknowledgement of her limitations as a poet. Of the many poems she must have written during these two years, only thirteen are extant and only four were published. While all four of the published poems were written in 1923, only "Enchanted" was published that year; the three others were published in 1924. Porter also translated and published in 1924 a sonnet by the seventeenth-century mystic Sor Juana Inés de la Cruz. Most of the remaining poems, unpublished but saved in letters or among her papers, were dated 1924 by Porter.

While Porter was organizing the issue for *Survey Graphic,* lining up contributors, and writing her own pieces, she was introduced to the poetry of Sor Juana Inés de la Cruz, possibly by the Chilean poet Gabriela Mistral.[33] Porter is likely to have translated Sor Juana's sonnet "To a Portrait of the Poet" soon afterward. "To a Portrait of the Poet" is a testament to the body's mortality and an indictment of art that deceives in its appearance of reality. Sor Juana's original sonnet was written in the Italian form with a rhyme scheme of *abbaabba cdcdcd.* Porter's translation does not fall readily into either the English or the Italian pattern, although in the structure of its content it is closer to the English. The concluding couplet defines the artist's motive, "an anxious diligence to preserve / A perishable thing," and judges the work of art, finally, as "a corpse, a whirl of dust, a shadow, nothing." Although Porter described her translation as a literal one, it is more than a mere rendering of words and approximating of syntax. Porter obviously considered the literary effectiveness of her translation to be as important as fidelity to the original content. In its physical form Porter's translation reveals her musical ear at its best and illustrates her ability to achieve rhythm with stressed syllables and skillfully to use near-rhyme, which replaced the full rhyme of the original.

Even more than Sor Juana's poetic skill, however, Sor Juana's legend would have appealed to Porter. In Porter's brief biographical sketch that accompanied the translation, she wrote: "Juana De Asbaje, in religion Sor Juana Inés de la Cruz, was, like most great spirits, at once the glory and the victim of her age. She was born in Mexico in 1651, of aristocratic Spanish parentage, and won the respect of the most advanced scholars of her time by her achievements in mathematics, astronomy, languages, and poetry. Her austere, impassioned and mystical

17

mind led her to the cloister, where she ended by renouncing her studies, and writing out her confession of faith in her own blood."

Porter would have seen irony in the sonnet whether Sor Juana intended it or not. In spite of the nun's charge that the work of art deceives in its "falsely reasoned arguments of colours," Sor Juana's art had survived her body's death more than two hundred years. The very existence of the sonnet underscored Porter's emerging views on the immortality of art, initially inspired by Keats and Yeats. Sor Juana's sonnet also related to Porter's evolving modern aesthetic of the rage for order. She later would write in a response to a question about the relationship between politics and art, "There are only two possibilities for any real order: in art and in religion."[34] Sor Juana's life and poetry had proved both possibilities.

"To a Portrait of the Poet" is the first of Porter's known translations. In 1952 Porter said she had read Ezra Pound's translations since they started appearing in 1915, and she is likely to have absorbed modern theories of translation in Greenwich Village in 1919–1920.[35] Porter probably saw in the poetry of Sor Juana an opportunity to participate in an important modernist exercise and to include in the *Survey Graphic* issue a remnant of Mexico's distinguished artistic past. It appeared in the Mexico number along with two other pieces written by Porter, "The Guild Spirit in Mexican Art" (an interview with Diego Rivera) and "Corridos," an essay about Mexican folk ballads.

As much as the translated Sor Juana sonnet, "Corridos" reveals Porter's notions about poetry and her aesthetic values as they had developed by 1923. In the essay, Porter describes the *corrido* as "the primitive, indigenous song of the Mexican people," "in effect, a ballad," and "a genuine folk poetry"—an acknowledgement of the relationship she saw between singing and poetry. Porter points out that even though the *corrido* is

18

informal, telling a story filled with seemingly irrelevant detail, the form is definitive: four lines to a verse, eight syllables to a line, and a refrain. Porter summarizes the word-of-mouth history of the *corrido,* its recent publication history (only the past twenty-five years),[36] its common subjects ("death, love, acts of vengeance, the appalling malignities of Fate"), its celebration of heroes, and its amazing air of realism even while graphically depicting the supernatural. Porter also observes the curious absence of a revolutionary corrido in spite of the fact that revolutionists are themselves celebrated in the songs as heroes. Porter explains the absence by noting that it is the heroic that fascinates the corrido singer, not revolutionary doctrine, and that "the maker of ballads" is "concerned with eternal verities." Her use of the word "maker" aligned her with the classical idea of the artist as craftsman, reaffirmed by Henry James and accepted by the moderns. Her declaration that pure art cannot be doctrinaire was a critical stand she was to take throughout her life and to illustrate in the best of her works.

Porter probably submitted most of the 1923–1924 poems to Rolfe Humphries and Genevieve Taggard, whom she may have met in Greenwich Village as early as 1919. In 1923 Humphries and Taggard were editors and among the founders of *The Measure: A Journal of Poetry.* From the poems Porter submitted (including several "witch" poems), the two editors accepted "Requiescat—" (retitled "Little Requiem" in *The Collected Essays and Occasional Writings of Katherine Anne Porter*) and two of the poems in "Three Songs from Mexico."[37] While Porter was putting together the pieces for *Survey Graphic,* she wrote "Requiescat—," published in the April 1924 issue of *The Measure.* It is a continuation of themes Porter had developed in her two published original stories and may well have been inspired by her reading and translating of Sor Juana's poetry. Like "Enchanted," "Requiescat—" is written in a ballad stanza, in which the short lines have patterns of syllabic stress that do not produce a designated meter. The first two quatrains present the problem, the last two a solution. The poem contains the phrase "the beaten dead," which appeared in "María Concepción" to describe María Rosa. The imagery evokes Joan of Arc ("she should have had . . . a scaled silver armour / For a breast cover") and a princess from chivalric romance ("she should have had the state / Of a king's daughter") but perhaps specifically Sor Juana. The "she" in the poem, an impersonal lyric, should have had the adulation due a heroine, but because she is an artist ("she had none of these / But a song instead"), she chooses (or has imposed on her) social death. The difference for Porter between Joan of Arc and Sor Juana would have been that Sor Juana had made art, whereas Joan, sanctified and idealized, had only become art. Porter could idolize them both, but she could identify with Sor Juana.

The poems in "Three Songs from Mexico," which Porter wrote near the end of the summer of 1923, depart from a ballad structure. They are, however, highly lyrical like the earlier poems. "In Tepozotlan" and "Fiesta de Santiago" constitute "Two Songs from Mexico," published in the January 1924 issue of *The Measure*. "In Tepozotlan" is based on a visit Porter made with the artist Winold Reiss to the Cathedral of Tepozotlan, about twenty-seven miles north of Mexico City.[38] The poem is a wistful lament for something or someone gone, represented by the "honey-colored girl dipping her arms shoulder-deep in the hives of honey," an image Porter already has used to characterize María Rosa in "María Concepción." The question "Who can tell me where she is gone?" is rhetorical; no one can explain the loss of innocence or youth, the vanishing of a golden age, or the disappearance of the idealized past of Mexico. The rhythm in this poem is less regular than that of Porter's early poems, and instead of easily identified iambic feet, Porter uses simple syllabic stress to achieve a musical effect, representing a still more sophisticated understanding of her older influences and at the same time falling in line with modern aesthetics.

"Fiesta de Santiago" is based on dances Porter witnessed at the feast of 25 July 1923.[39] In its images of a dancer in "a wild delicate dance" the poem corresponds to Porter's essay "The Fiesta of Guadalupe," in which Porter refers to "the sight of men dancing in a religious ecstasy." The poem is based on paradox that points to the themes of several of the essays and most of the fiction set in Mexico: the coexistence of the primitive and the civilized, the past and the present, and death and life. In this poem Porter combines images in arresting ways ("the odour of silence") and uses alliteration skillfully ("delicate"/ "dance"/"dream"/"death") to produce a musical effect. The end rhymes are irregular (*aabcdecfgf*), but Porter uses assonance to intensify the rhythm and bind lines together. The precise syntax of the four sentences that comprise the poem reveals Porter's careful craftsmanship. "He" is the subject of the first, second, and fourth sentences. The subject of the third sentence is "the odour of silence," drawing the reader's attention to the dramatic synaesthesis, a distinctive trait of modern, symbolist poetry, especially that of Baudelaire and Rimbaud.[40]

"Remembering Cuernavaca," the poem in the original "Three Poems from Mexico" that Humphries and Taggard did not accept for *The Measure,* was intended by Porter to be placed between the other two. Not so finely crafted as the other two poems in the suite (the "weaving sand" image especially unsuccessful), the Cuernavaca poem addresses the relationship between reality and dreams (or memory) or between reality and imagination. Unlike the other two poems, "Remembering Cuernavaca" is only implicitly about death, embedded in Porter's image of the "greedy sun," drawn loosely again from Shakespeare's "Fear No More the Heat of the Sun."

On 12 August 1923, Porter had visited Cuernavaca with Robert Haberman, a socialist lawyer and head of the Foreign

Language Department of the Ministry of Education, and two women from the Mexican Feminist Council. Porter, whose enthusiasm for the revolution had waned, was to attend with them an official observance of agricultural progress in the region. In impressionistic notes she made about the trip, Porter muses that perhaps she should have been discussing sugar and rice crops with the governor but instead, responding to the beauty of the town, she "sat under a blooming bougainvillea and plucked . . . a bouquet of sweet blowing grass."[41] The conflict between political reality and the higher truth of art lies behind the poem. In "Remembering Cuernavaca" Porter was unable to translate her perception of that conflict into effective poetic language.

When Porter sent Taggard the witch poems in 1924, she said they had been written while she was still in Mexico, thus before the end of October 1923.[42] In subject and form they are noticeably at variance with the other poems she had been writing in 1923, but they are similar in significant ways to her stories "Virgin Violeta" and the unpublished "The Lovely Legend," both of which she was working on in late 1923 and early 1924. The stories and the witch poems were inspired by Porter's affair with Salomón de la Selva of 1921 or 1922. Her return to Mexico in 1923 must have resurrected the emotions she had suppressed when the affair ended. The witch poems as well as "Virgin Violeta" and "The Lovely Legend" are filled with hatred.[43]

Although Porter routinely replaced love with hate when a romance soured, her tendency was to suppress the bad memories and refer to past lovers (or husbands) only rarely—and then, obliquely. De la Selva was the exception. Not only did Porter mention him by name for many years; she voiced particular loathing for him, using him as the model for the odious Carlos, a poet, in "Virgin Violeta" and for Amado, an unscrupulous sentimentalist, in "The Lovely Legend."[44] If "Enchanted" reflects some of Porter's worries about the devastating effect of romantic entanglements on her art, the witch poems reflect her bitterness after the fact.

"This Transfusion" is a witch's curse on a betraying lover. Although the poem reveals Porter's attention to musical patterns, Taggard rejected it on the grounds that it was "unfinished."[45] Taggard said the same about "Witch's Song," which is more sophisticated than "This Transfusion" and represents more complex emotions than simple hate. "Witch's Song" contains enigmatic images that combine themes of maternity, birth, betrayal, and death. The image of "scared green faces" may have a meaning personal to Porter, but other statements and phrases such as "a witch and the water / Are bound with a tie—are mother and daughter" are clarified in light of Porter's suppressed feelings about the death of her own mother. Her guilt over her failure to bear a child (profoundly apparent in "Flowering Judas"), her unresolved grief for her mother, and her hatred for the betraying lover join together in this poem.

Porter wrote another witch poem that she called "Ordeal by Ploughshare."[46] Undated, the manuscript has typed on it a Greenwich Village address (18 Jones Street), one among several places Porter lived in New York in the 1920s.[47] "Ordeal by Ploughshare" has images in it that link it to Porter's unfinished story "The Pincess" and specifically to "Virgin Violeta," a story treating the modernist theme of the Apollonian and Dionysian conflict. The story focuses on fourteen-year-old Violeta, who has a romantic view of life. Violeta cannot reconcile what she has been taught at the convent ("modesty, chastity, silence, obedience, with a little French and music and some arithmetic") with the dark truths she is intuiting in her predatory cousin, Carlos. Violeta's romanticism expresses itself in a fantasizing about a perpetually festive future and in her hiding Carlos's poems in her missal to read during mass so that "the thrilling music of strange words" will drown "the chorus of bell and choir." Violeta loves best Carlos's poem about the ghosts of nuns returning to the ruins of their convent and "dancing in the moonlight with the shades of lovers forbidden them in life, treading with bared feet on broken glass as a penance for their loves." When Carlos, his eyes "bright and shallow, almost like the eyes of Pepe, the macaw," tries to kiss Violeta, she "is angry with all her might." After the anger comes disillusionment, "a painful unhappiness" (32), and a rejection of both charity, represented by the convent, and cupidity, represented by Carlos. Violeta, to amuse herself, occasionally makes "ugly caricatures of Carlos." The repudiation of extremes, followed by a retreat to a state of detachment, is a theme Porter develops in her fictional works, notably in "Theft," the Miranda cycle, "The Leaning Tower," and *Ship of Fools*.

"Ordeal by Ploughshare" is filled with conventional symbols from Gothic romance. It is a song telling a story about a romantic dream similar to the romantic poem written by Carlos in "Virgin Violeta." Just as Violeta's silently reading the poem at mass blocks out "bell and choir," the persona of "Ordeal by Ploughshare" weeps when she hears "the crying / Of an old bell" because it brings forth the dream that contains "solemn singing" and "the wind-blown clangour" of a "mad bell." The most dramatic similarities between Carlos's poem and "Ordeal by Ploughshare" are the common images of blood, ghosts, and dancing on broken glass, altered in "Ordeal by Ploughshare" to walking on sharp blades. In contrast, however, to the nuns who dance with joy in Carlos's poem, the "thin changeling creature" in Porter's poem is joyless, facing death alone. The "harsh bitter crying" is her own. The poem is personal to Porter, who said that in her childhood she believed herself to be a "changeling."[48] The poem's similarity to "Virgin Violeta" makes it likely to be an expression of Porter's emotional state at the end of the De la Selva affair.

The last two poems Porter supposedly wrote in 1923 and 1924 were both untitled, a song she later called "Now No Spring" (see Appendix) and a lyric included in a letter to Francisco Aguilera, a Chilean doctoral student at Yale with whom Porter began a brief romantic alliance after her return from Mexico.[49] In its original form, "Now No Spring" is a lyric expressing an unspecified personal grief. The first stanza describes nature's response ("a green leaf" and "a ploughed furrow") to human grief ("tears" and "sorrow"), implying hope in the seasons' cyclic renewal of life. In the second stanza, the persona asks which spring or summer will alleviate her pain. The poem is unpolished with awkward rhythms and imprecise rhymes that only approximate an *aabbccddd* scheme.

In 1943 Porter revised the poem, which she referred to only as a "song," underscoring its lyrical nature, and gave it the title "Now No Spring," the title indicating a shift in mood. Still not technically flawless, the later version is nevertheless smoother than the original. Porter replaced the opening line's "*my* tears" and "*my* grief" with "*early* tears" and "*child's* grief" and the third line's "*my* tears" and "*my* sorrow" with "*young* grief" and "*early* sorrow" (emphases mine), moving the perspective from the purely personal to the impersonal. The verb tense is changed from the present ("spring sends," "summer brings") to the conditional ("spring would send") and simple past ("summer brought"). In the later version the persona is looking backwards, whereas in the original version the persona is commenting on a present condition. Porter also replaced "green" (modifying "leaf") with "shapely," and "ploughed" (modifying "furrow") with "ripened"—shifts from the common and literal to the unexpected and figurative.

The most significant revision occurs in the second stanza. There the persona, who in the earlier draft wonders how long before the grief is lifted ("what spring shall set me free"), is

25

resigned to permanent grief, declaring, "Now no spring can set me free." The two versions of the poem show how Porter's expectations for personal happiness have changed in the intervening nineteen years, during which she has gone through at least two more marriages and numerous love affairs and has passed fifty years of age. Even with the critical adulation she was receiving by 1943, Porter's emotional pain, tied to her fruitless search for love and security, would not be alleviated. The last line, unmusical in its original "rough awakened scars," becomes the alliterative "winter-wakened scars" and anticipates images and themes of Porter's last poems and fictional pieces.

[Lights on the river] is a more effective poem than "Now No Spring," although there is no evidence that Porter ever worked further on it or submitted it for publication. Its twelve lines of free verse are bound together with varied metaphors and images of sharpness—daggers, the cutting edges of houses, stones.[50] By such internal figures and mood it can be linked to "Virgin Violeta" and "Ordeal by Ploughshare."

It was at the end of 1924, the year in which the greatest number of Porter's poems were published, that she concluded she was, after all, not really a poet. She told Taggard, "I realize more and more that I am a prose writer: verse is a strange, always experimental form with me. But I love it, and shall probably keep on experimenting from time to time."[51] Although Porter continued to write and translate poems and published some of them, her creative interest was focused on her prose fiction. And with the publication in 1924 of Porter's poems in *The Measure*, "Virgin Violeta" in *Century*, and her three pieces in *Survey Graphic*, except for working sporadically on "Flowering Judas" and reviewing books about Mexicans and Mexico, Porter turned her attention for most of the remainder of the decade to her own country and cultural roots. She did not write any more fiction about Mexico until she finished "Flowering Judas" in 1929. Although in 1930 she translated verses from a

Mexican folk dance, she appears never to have composed another poem that was specifically inspired by Mexico or particular persons she had met there.

In the fall of 1926 Porter wrote two related poems—"Winter Burial," which was published in the *New York Herald Tribune*," and "November in Windham," which was not published until 1955, in *Harper's*.[52] Both poems grew out of Porter's sojourns in Connecticut in 1924 and 1926. In 1924 Porter stayed in North Windham with a group of writers and artists. In 1926 she lived in the Merryall Valley with a young art student named Ernest Stock, to whom Porter may have been briefly married.[53] Josephine Herbst and John Hermann, among other friends, lived nearby. The group spent some pleasant days together, farming modestly and enjoying one another's company, but Stock grew tedious and Porter grew bored and miserable. Her disappointment in Stock and the cold of the approaching winter had made her discontent. Porter wrote the poems and returned to New York. The tone of the poems, like Porter's mood, is somber and bleak as she exploits the traditional symbolism of winter as a season of death and sterility.

"Winter Burial" is a slight, impressionistic poem of two four-line stanzas, the first a description of the season and the second an imperative to bury a seed that presumably will flower after the winter's days have been "tapped out upon a clock." "November in Windham" begins with a reference to Martinmas, a feast day (November 11) celebrating the end of autumn and the beginning of winter. With a five-line stanzaic structure that is new for Porter, the poem is more ambitious and more lyrical than "Winter Burial." It resembles a common Spanish form that limits each strophe to two consecutive rhymes with the restriction that no stanza can end in a couplet (Porter's pattern of *abcca* is repeated in each stanza). Since it also is a variation of a ballad stanza, it resembles as well poems by some of her favorite poets of the past such as Sidney, Herbert, and Poe. The persona poses no cosmic question, establishes no noticeable irony, but rather projects her own winter-dread onto the very countryside "aching at the core, / Dead-tired of the year's labors, weary beyond sleep." Evocative, this mood piece is sustained by descriptive images that are more literal than figurative. Like others of her poems from this period, it is written in the spirit of Rimbaud and Valéry.

When Porter was writing the two poems, she was also trying to finish three stories. One of them was a story about an Irish woman who created a scandal by adopting young boys for questionable reasons. At the time, Porter thought of calling her story "St. Martin's Summer," a reference to the late spell of fine weather that traditionally occurred around Martinmas. She characterized the theme of her story as "a season of false warmth."[54] The story was not completed until 1932, and Porter called it "The Cracked Looking-Glass."[55] In the meantime, in the autumn of 1928, Porter met Matthew Josephson and began another sure-to-fail love affair that would bring forth more poetry.

The surviving two Josephson poems written at the beginning and end of the affair are very different from one another. "First Episode" is more experimental, more modern, than any poem Porter had written before. In free verse, the love poem celebrates a tentative union, but the persona, the lyrical "I," is anxious because "this is a perilous place." More abstract and general than earlier poems, "First Episode" has only a few symbolic images, the most effective ones in the stanza that contains "a curse on all wounding things," cataloged with anaphora. The last two lines, "Let us breathe innerly without stir / Lest a leaf shake and arouse the sleeper," are reminiscent of the last two lines of T. S. Eliot's "The Love Song of J. Alfred Prufrock": "We have lingered in the chambers of the sea / By sea-girls wreathed with seaweed red and brown / Till human voices wake us and we drown." Porter's poem, however, is truly a love poem and, while melancholy and gloomy, holds an element of hope that is absent in Eliot's. Hope is the element within her personality that sustained her numerous but futile attempts to find a lasting romantic relationship.

"Morning Song," written at the end of the affair, reveals Porter's usual reaction to the disillusionment that attends the failure of romantic love. What is unusual in this poem is that the persona is the jilting lover. Instead of bringing forth the personally experienced pain of being betrayed, Porter had to imagine the callous arrogance of the faithless lover. For the effect of irony, she reverted to a conventional Cavalier beginning suggestive of Marlowe or Herrick ("Come, my laid lady, whom I wooed with words, / And called my Star—"), which in this instance quickly turns to a contrasting bitterness. The depth of feeling in this poem is not so intense as that in the witch poems. Here, the motivating emotion is more evidently self-disgust for being deceived than it is blatant hatred.

During the affair with Josephson, Porter's ever-frail health broke, and a group of friends made it possible for her to have a restorative sojourn in Bermuda. Porter sailed for Bermuda in early March, depressed over the apparent end of her affair with Josephson. It was while Porter was in Bermuda—where she completed eleven chapters of her Cotton Mather biography and the story "Theft"—that she was inspired to write two poems, "Night Blooming Cereus" and "West Indian Island." The story and the poems reflect her state of mind at the time. Although both poems on the surface are impressionistic depictions of place, latent meanings are revealed to make them much more.

"Night Blooming Cereus" is written in Porter's comfortable four-line ballad stanza. She experiments with enjambment at the end of the first quatrain and within the lines of the second. The final stanza has end stops, creating an orderliness that conforms to the content as the day progresses to evening, which brings together "all that bright morning scattered." The poem, however, is insufficiently thought through, with the movement unnaturally abrupt from dawn to evening. The image of the child returning to his mother seems outside the focus of the poem, two thirds of which is devoted to describing the night. In handwritten notes on an early draft of the poem, Porter explains the poem's meaning: "almost literally it is: Night brings together again all that the morning separated—the sheep, the goats, and the child to his mother." Certain aspects of this poem anticipate later works. Porter's use of a flower as a focusing symbol anticipates "Flowering Judas" (which Porter was thinking about if not working on in Bermuda in 1929), and the child's returning to his mother anticipates a theme that was forming powerfully in Porter's creative psyche.

"West Indian Island" is the most ambitious poem Porter had attempted before 1930. Immediately apparent is its source in "Night Blooming Cereus," Porter retaining the initial line of the earlier poem with its contrasting images of savage thorns and a delicate flower. The three parts of "West Indian Island" represent an expansion of the parts of the English sonnet.[56] Porter had told Taggard in 1924 that she was working on a sonnet sequence, and while there is no evidence that she produced a finished sonnet during these years in the mid to late twenties, she was studying the form whose influence began to be apparent in some of her fiction published in the 1930s. "The Grave," for example, condensed as it is, can be broken into two roughly equal parts with the concluding paragraph, separated from the internal chronology of the story by twenty years, functioning like the concluding couplet of a sonnet. The same structure, although lengthened, forms the matrix of "Old Mortality" and "Noon Wine." *Ship of Fools,* which was evolving in these years as a novel in progress, is divided into three parts. Reinforcing Porter's preference for a tripartite structure in her fiction were also such classics beloved by Porter as *The Divine Comedy.*

The first part of "West Indian Island" has no subtitle and is nearly three times as long as either of the other two parts. The impersonal, third-person description of the island becomes entangled with a description of the psychological landscape of the persona, who pleads with the island to restore her to a "familiar country." The poem's second part, subtitled "The Hurricane" (the brewing storm obliquely referred to in the first part), includes a dialogue between God, "straddling the whirlwind," and the speaker, who, using language reminiscent of Emily Dickinson, grants to God what belongs to God (the firmament and the seas) but declares that "what is mine I keep."[57] The poem's final part, subtitled "Recession," contains an explanation of the boldness of the persona, who challenges God. The encounter was after all a "contest with a mythical God." In the aftermath of the storm, the speaker identifies with "the broken armed trees" and poses finally another Blakean question: who shall explain, apologize, to the frogs and birds who were killed by the storm? The question is another version of "Who weaponed me with melting flesh[?]" ("Song with Castanet Accompaniment") or "Who can tell me where she is gone?" ("In Tepozotlan"). In a note Porter scrawled at the bottom of one of the two early drafts of the poem, she explained the subject as "this lost cause," and the theme as "all things created" are "destroyed again without explanation." She says that she stands with such things: "We shall fall together."[58]

The entire poem is Porter's honest expression of her inner turmoil as she passed her thirty-ninth birthday 15 May 1929. A week afterward she wrote to Josephine Herbst that she had no lover and could not imagine finding one, but she didn't want to continue having miserable affairs which left her feeling as if she had "just got out of a hurricane."[59] Porter's depression grew not only out of her disquieting loneliness as she approached the age of forty but also out of her concern over the precarious state of her health and her yearning for a "place" where she would be welcomed and called "Daughter"—in order words, a yearning for home. It is the beginning articulation of a theme that would find expression in her most exquisite poem and in her only long novel. In the meantime, she had to be content with a sibling relationship to a natural world she only partly understood.

Porter's early drafts of "West Indian Island," which she dated Bermuda 1929, reveal for the most part only minor changes in words (see Appendix). In every instance, however, Porter's changes improve the poem. But even in its last version, Porter wondered whether the poem was finished. She sent a copy to Eugene Pressly in 1933 when she was in Paris and he was in Spain. She asked him what he thought of it but told him that as she copied it over she saw that it was not yet a poem but "only the theme for one."[60] She must have thought otherwise later, however, because she discussed offering the poem as it was to Malcolm Cowley for the *New Republic* or to Eugene Jolas for *transition*.[61]

Like most of the poems Porter wrote in the 1920s and afterward, this one shows the influence of poems from earlier centuries and also of modern poetry, particularly that of the symbolist poets. The movement from the external to the internal, a feature of much symbolist poetry, is confirmed by Porter here. In the letter to Pressly, Porter described the progression of thought as "from the external scene withinward" and says that she will expand it within the form it has. A subject outline she made for the poem illustrates her concept of its structure:

Scene
Day and Night
Statement
Challenge to Calm [replaces "Invocation," marked out]
The Answer [replaces "Hurricane," marked out]
Recession
Song

Of the seven divisions, four of them—"Scene," "Day and Night," "Statement," and "Challenge to Calm"—are to be found in the first part. "Invocation," replaced by "Challenge to Calm," refers to lines 26 through 40, which begin "O Island, loosen your roots, take to the sea." "The Answer" was her characterization of the hurricane, and "Song" refers to the rhetorical question with which the poem ends.

"West Indian Island" has relevance to other works of Porter's. The image and symbol of the tree frogs link the poem to Porter's story "The Fig Tree," the first draft of which she completed during her stay in Bermuda.[62] One of the primary symbols in the story, the symbol on which the story turns, is the tree frogs' announcing rain with a "weep, weep" sound, which the child Miranda, Porter's autobiographical character, has misunderstood, thinking it a crying sound made by a baby chicken she has buried, having presumed it dead. In this poem Porter also uses an image she will use later to describe herself: "This shape that sits in famished pride."

Porter's disenchantment with Bermuda is apparent in "West Indian Island," and at the end of the summer, she left for New York. She rented a room in the house of friends in Brooklyn, and she began to think more and more of Mexico, perhaps because of its similarities and contrasts to Bermuda. For the next few months she wrote book reviews to earn money—among the books, works about Mexico which rekindled her memories of that country to the extent that she was able to finish "Flowering Judas," the story establishing her fame.[63]

In the early spring of 1930 Porter developed again the chronic bronchial ailment that had sent her to Bermuda. And again, friends rescued her, contributing money to support her for a year in Mexico. Thus in April of 1930 Porter returned to one of her "familiar countries" (Texas being another) for which she had voiced yearning in "West Indian Island." For the next year and a half, she again became involved in the social life of Mexico, although the social scene was very different from what she had left in the fall of 1923. Porter was working on the long novel she had been thinking about for several years, she wrote an essay on Mexico, and she reviewed two books by Kay Boyle.[64] The only poem she produced during this time in Mexico was a folk song she translated for *Mexican Folkways* soon after her arrival. "Music of the Official Jarabe and Versos" was an exercise in appreciation of Mexico's folk tradition and an acknowledgement of Porter's return to an important segment of her past. The residue of her Mexican inspiration would be worked out in fiction. After "Flowering Judas," she produced two more stories set in Mexico, "Hacienda" (1932) and "That Tree" (1934), and she set the opening pages of *Ship of Fools* in Vera Cruz.

The year 1931 marked another turning point in Porter's life. With the critical praise following the publication of her first collection of stories had come a Guggenheim Fellowship for her first trip to Europe. She had passed age forty and still had not found a lasting love, although the man who traveled to Europe with her, Eugene Dove Pressly, represented her then-current hope. The first piece Porter wrote in Europe was "Bouquet for October," a poem about the early European phase of her relationship with Gene Pressly, whom she had met in 1930 in Mexico. Although Porter married Pressly in 1933, the poem, which Porter dated "Berlin, September 27, 1931," is wrapped in an air of melancholy that anticipates the later unhappiness of the marriage. The poem contains themes and techniques apparent in Porter's poems from the earliest "Texas: By the Gulf of Mexico" through "November in Windham," "Now No Spring," and "West Indian Island."

Eight stanzas of irregular lineation, "Bouquet for October" is lyrical and impressionistic. Like the narrative voice of "November in Windham," the persona sets forth in the first stanza the poem's theme that the spring-born (both Porter's and Pressly's birthdays were in May) always suffer and grieve during the winter months and can only wait for the next spring. The speaker suggests that attempts to define love are as futile as arguments to define heroics, especially as such arguments regard "Statesmen"—with Porter making a subtle comment about changing fashions in politics as she recently had done not so subtly in a letter to Paul O'Higgins and in her story "Theft."[65]

The poem's seventh stanza, which in the manuscript Porter labeled "Refrain," begins with a repetition of the first line of the poem, "This is not our season, the spring born." In a marginal note, Porter wrote beside the last three lines, "Once more from the beginning"—illustrating again the degree to which she thought of her poems as songs. With only minor changes, the poem was published in the winter 1932–1933 edition of *Pagany* (see Appendix). When Porter revised and expanded this poem more than twenty-five years later, she renamed it "After a Long Journey" and made explicit some of the oblique points in the earlier version.

When Porter and Pressly moved to Paris in 1932, the money from the Guggenheim was dwindling, Pressly's diplomatic work was uncertain and erratic, and they frequently worried about money. In Paris, Porter renewed acquaintance with Ford Madox

Ford and Eugene Jolas, among others. Through Ford, she met Monroe Wheeler, Glenway Wescott, and Barbara Harrison. Wheeler and Harrison had established a small publishing house, Harrison of Paris, and published short-run editions of attractively produced volumes. Knowing that Porter needed money, Ford had suggested to Porter that she translate a selection of medieval French songs for a book Wheeler and Harrison were considering putting together. In a letter to Porter of 3 March 1932, Wheeler confirmed that Porter had agreed to translate fifteen French popular songs by 1 May 1932, for the sum of three thousand francs.[66] But Porter had considerable difficulty translating the songs and at one point wrote Harrison that she would have to renege on the agreement.[67] When Wheeler found a person to help with the translations, however, Porter was able to create melodious and poetic English versions.[68] The volume that was eventually produced in 1933 was *Katherine Anne Porter's French Song-Book*, a collection of seventeen songs in both the original French and Porter's modern English translation. Bars of music were included to show the melody to which the songs were sung. Of as great interest to the Porter scholar and other admirers of her work are Porter's charming introductions, which contain the expected clarity, wit, and brilliant turn of phrase that characterize the best of her writing, both fiction and nonfiction, including her poetry.

During the time Porter was working on the translations of the *French Song-Book*, she translated a poem by Clément Marot, a "Song" that was not included in the *Song-Book*. Her comments about it in letters to Glenway Wescott and Monroe Wheeler reveal the kind of attention she gave to translation. In November of 1933 Porter wrote to Wheeler responding to his suggestion that she send some poetry to Russell Lynes at *Harper's Bazaar*. She says she might send Lynes some translations from Centenaire or one by Clément Marot that she has started to translate as the following:

> I am no more what once I was,
> And what I was no more shall be,
> My merry spring and summer days
> Have taken careless leave of me.

"The trouble is," Porter wrote, "Marot's verse has alternate feminine rhymes which adds a muted syllable when sung, and I haven't got yet."[69] Nine months later, she sent Wheeler and Glenway Wescott a copy of the original French of Marot's poem to go with her translation, which she had already given them. She wrote, "Well, you see what a lovely arrangement of rimes riche alternating with feminine rhymes it is, and my translation has no such deftness. I think the English version sings, just the same." She promised to send music for it when she found it.[70]

Porter's struggle with the last two lines of the first stanza and her final revision illustrate her concept of translation. A nearly literal translation would have been "My beautiful spring and my summer / Have jumped through the window." Her first rendition, unsatisfactory to her, retained an adjective with "spring," and she translated the fourth line into a nearly literal statement, the trope existing only in the personification of spring and summer. Porter's final revision gives the adjective to "summer," as she reverses the sequence of the seasons, and she places in the final line of the stanza a metaphor, "thieves farewell," representing the kind of impersonal departure she interpreted Marot's original French to convey. Porter was not able to produce either *rime riche* or feminine rhyme in the English translation, the Germanic roots of English naturally asserting themselves. She had to content herself with masculine rhymes in the second and fourth lines of the two stanzas (Marot's second stanza has alternating masculine and feminine rhymes) following the rule of Saint-Gelais and Ronsard to alternate masculine and feminine rhymes. Porter was familiar with the tradition behind *rime riche* and the variations in combinations of masculine and feminine rhyme from Spenser and Shakespeare through Wyatt, Peele, Chapman, and Donne and to moderns such as Baudelaire and Eliot. When the final push came to choose between fidelity to the metrics and literal sense of the original or achieving a musicality with an approximation of the content, she chose the latter, as she consistently had done.

In 1933 Porter also wrote a poem that was uncharacteristic of her and a violation of her stand on the separation of art and politics. Never published, the poem was titled "Liberals" and dated by Porter as "166 Boulevard Montparnasse, Paris, 1933." It is an openly political diatribe, and Porter may have been exercising her art only in an attempt to get a nettlesome idea off her mind. Certainly she had strong ideas about politics, but usually she reserved such polemics for nonfiction, that is, letters, essays, or book reviews. Long before 1933 Porter had come to view extreme political positions with distaste, and while her sympathies generally tended more toward liberalism (when forced to choose categories, she described herself politically as a "liberal Democrat"), from time to time she was as disenchanted with liberals as she was the "fascist-minded." Her years in between-the-wars Paris were such a period.

"Liberals" is a loosely structured poem of four *abcb* stanzas in which alliteration is the primary musical feature. Two metaphors and several allusions constitute the figurative language of the poem. Life is represented by "goldfish or quicksilver," and apathy is represented by "a soft land." Allusions to a medieval carol ("Sumer is icumen in"), Psalm 107, and Shakespeare's *Richard III* and *Henry IV, Part II* establish a standard which the "liberals" badly fail to meet. It is high irony and a technique for satire that Porter will develop fully in *Ship of Fools*.[71]

While Porter was still in Paris, she wrote a finely crafted poem inspired by Freud, whom she had read since the 1920s when his *A General Introduction to Psychoanalysis* appeared in English translation. Although she was to attack Freud on specific moral grounds, she undoubtedly was influenced by his ideas in general, even paraphrasing passages from *A General Introduction to Psychoanalysis* for inclusion in *Ship of Fools.* "Measures for Song and Dance" incorporates some of the poetic techniques Porter had developed or acquired over the years, but it also represents a departure from the lyric and ballad forms that dominate her poetry canon. The subject of the poem is the cycle of mythic patterns that human beings relive (according to both Freud and Jung). It was a subject that required a patterned vehicle, and Porter created an intricate one to underscore the thematic affirmation of the subject.[72]

Porter employs in "Measures for Song and Dance" techniques that she drew from the poetics of Eliot, Pound, and other moderns. The tone of the poem is ironic, nearly that of a mock epic. The language is conversational, and Porter's wit is particularly evident in such colloquialisms as "gorged to the ears" and in humanizing characterizations of God and other figures in the Edenic myth. She echoes themes in others of her works: the playing out of primitive forces in "María Concepción," and the fecklessness and faithlessness of males in all the stories set in Mexico, in the witch poems, and in such stories as "Theft" and "The Jilting of Granny Weatherall" and in *Ship of Fools.* The resourcefulness and manipulativeness of Eve and Lilith are no match for the deterministic power of cyclic enactment of myth abetted by the weakness of men. Except for *Ship of Fools,* "Measures for Song and Dance" is the final expression of the mythic feminism that pervades much of Porter's canon.

In February of 1936 Porter made a trip to the United States to do research in Boston on her Cotton Mather biography and to visit her family in Texas. In the summer, she went back to Paris in order to make the return trip to the United States with Pressly. The trip she made alone seems peculiar in light of her and Pressly's planned departure from Paris only a few months later. But Porter's trip of February 1936 was timed to extend through her own forty-sixth birthday, on 15 May. On that day she visited the grave of her mother. According to various autobiographical accounts of the visit, she wrote a poem on the occasion and buried it in the earth of her mother's grave.[73] The poem, eventually titled "Anniversary in a Country Cemetery," expresses Porter's identification of "home" with the grave, of her physical self with her mother's "dust," and of her lifelong emotional pain with her grief over the death of her mother. Implicit in the poem is Porter's profound regret that by failing to have a child she has violated the female principle which her mother symbolized and which Porter herself idealized. Porter no doubt hoped the pilgrimage would alleviate her pain and would bring her solace.

Before Porter visited the grave, she had drafted a poem that she titled "Time Has Heaped a Bitter Dust." Expressing the core ideas in the first drafts of the "Anniversary" poem, "Time Has Heaped a Bitter Dust" can be read in the abstract as a philosophical statement about the relationship between the living and the dead. More specifically, the poem is about Porter's mother and the effect of her death on Porter. The "she" of the poem is Mary Alice Jones Porter, whose death in 1892 had devastated Porter's father, Harrison Boone (Harry) Porter, and, consequently, his children. According to Porter's accounts of her childhood, time did not alleviate her father's grief but only made it bitter.[74] Although Harry's mother moved her son and his four children in with her, Porter always felt the absence of the mother she never knew but imagined to be gentler than the stern disciplinarian who took her place.

The first two stanzas of "Time Has Heaped a Bitter Dust" define the boundaries within which "she" lived her life, marriage (represented by the hearth) and motherhood (represented by the cradle). The narrative voice shifts from the impersonal to the personal, in the third stanza becoming the lyrical "I" who explains herself in the terms of the idealized mother's boundaries. Instead of tending a hearth, the alienated and dissatisfied "I" has been nomadic ("I take all roads and each road / Is strange to me"), compelled to keep moving in time and space ("Still I fly before the winds / And the staring sun"). At a particular time of the year, however, the "she" of the poem calls to her side the poem's persona, self-described in the concluding line as "this prodigal shape of her pain." In "West Indian Island," Porter had her persona refer to herself as "this shape that sits in famished pride" and that yearns for a "familiar country" which will not mock her journeys but will welcome her as "Daughter." In 1936, Porter made a symbolic effort to satisfy that yearning.

"Time Has Heaped a Bitter Dust" is built on a series of metaphors, the metonymies in the concluding couplet especially modern and arresting. "Her dust remembers its dust" is both material (in the sense of one of Aristotle's "four causes") and reductive, as Porter's friend Kenneth Burke used the term to refer to incorporeal and corporeal tropes.[75] The mother's literal dust attracts the still-living but mortal dust (that is, one who will be dust in the course of time) to her side. The mother's dust is a metonymy that represents the physical mother (it is all that remains of her total physical being), but in its personification (it "remembers" and "calls again"), it becomes a metaphor for instinctual maternal love—a theme Porter treats notably in "María Concepción" and extensively in *Ship of Fools*. The final metaphor in the poem, "this prodigal shape of her pain," combines the concepts of waywardness and the pain of childbirth. The child is the material product of that pain, a manifestation of its having existed in time. This child, "this shape," is that of the persona Porter created to represent herself.

According to notes Porter made in 1967 on a manuscript version of the "Anniversary" poem, she had been taken away from the house when her mother died and had never returned there or seen her mother's grave until she made the pilgrimage in 1936, forty-four years, two months, and thirteen days after the death, according to Porter's marginal calculations. The version Porter identified as having been written at the graveside is untitled (see Appendix).[76]

Another version, which Porter called "Birthday in a Country Cemetery," was probably written during the same period. Noticeable is the shift to past tense verbs, line rearrangements that produce enjambment, and word changes: in the third line the adjective modifying "house" is changed from "fallen" to "sunken" (making "house" a referent to the literal homestead, which was gone, and the grave, which was literally sunken). The adjective modifying "dust" is changed from "drowsing" to "patient." The fourth line, "*Where I* sit at *the* door," becomes "*There to* sit at *her* door" (emphases mine).

Porter created still another version of the poem for her journal (dated summer 1936). All these early, short versions of the poem include the kernel ideas of "Time Has Heaped a Bitter Dust," which stops with the observation that the memory of the mother (the mother's ghost) pulls the child to her side at a particular time of year. The three early versions still do not explain the significance of "this time of year" or identify it by season or month. In notes Porter made with the journal entry, she says that on her first visit she was shaking all the way there "with fear of my own feelings." But the experience was more than comforting, as Porter describes it: "When I first caught sight of the quiet dark blue marble stone, and the old calm weathered earth of her grave, I sat down beside her and began instantly to dig a place to plant the rosebush I had brought. I felt strangely at home, rested, eased, full of the most profound almost painful joy."[77]

"Anniversary in a Country Cemetery" appeared in *Harper's Bazaar* in 1940 only slightly changed from the first manuscript version. Porter's original sixth line of her eight-line verse was

"Her dust remembers its dust and calls again." In the first published version, the line is broken after the second "dust," with "And calls again" creating a separate line and making the poem a nine-line verse. The change is for the better because the new line with its two iambic feet is closer in meter to the two feet (one iambic and one anapestic) of the final line, with which it rhymes.

By 1956 Porter had revised the poem again, resurrecting the "Birthday" version and expanding it by two lines, the new lines offering reconciliation that goes a step beyond being "welcomed" home, as in the 1940 and earlier versions. As she was inclined to do in her fiction, Porter had allowed the distance of time to work on memory to give a final shape to her artistic vision.[78] The memory of the rosebush Porter had planted at her mother's grave in 1936 provided still another variation on "dust." During Porter's childhood, dried flowers, preferably roses, were often tucked away with keepsakes, and Porter used such dust of flowers as symbols of the dead past and sweet memories of it.[79] In the two added lines, Porter creates an appositive, "this shape of her love," to rename "this shape of her pain." Now the child who was the manifestation of the mother's birthing pain is also the manifestation of the mother's love. The child, still mortal, is "living dust" who encloses (and causes to make live) the mother's love, which is "sweet as the dust of roses." Porter revised the poem a final time for inclusion in *The Collected Essays and Occasional Writings*. She divided the two lines into three and changed the clause "whose living dust encloses her love" to "whose living dust reposes / Beside her dust," concluding the poem with the controlling image of the visit to the cemetery.

Whatever personal reconciliation Porter achieved with her 1936 visit to her mother's grave, her new-found equilibrium did not include sanguinity about her marriage to Pressly. When they returned together to the United States in the autumn of

43

1936, they began to live apart more than together. Although they were not legally divorced until the spring of 1938, the marriage was effectively over by 1936. Porter settled in New York, renewed old friendships, finished her short novel "Noon Wine," and joined the League of American Writers. Although she was momentarily attracted again to the liberalism and the bohemianism of New York, by the end of the year she was complaining that all her old friends in New York had "turned Communist" and were "trying to convert" her. She said they used "all the arguments" she had given them in 1924–1927 but that "they have forgotten all about that."[80]

In spite of Porter's preferred apolitical stance, she was drawn into a movement sympathetic to the Loyalists in the Spanish Civil War. Rolfe Humphries, who with Genevieve Taggard had accepted Porter's poems for *The Measure,* asked Porter to translate two Spanish ballads for a collection of Spanish Civil War poetry to be published by Vanguard Press. Humphries wrote Porter 9 June 1937, to "jog her elbow a bit" regarding the two ballads.[81] He said he was supposed to take them to the printers and would leave room for hers. A week later, he telegraphed Porter: "Can you have Spanish ballads at League office Friday morning urgent Thank you."[82] Porter produced one ballad, titled "The Olive Grove," translated from an original ballad by R. Beltran Logroño. It appeared in the volume titled . . . *and Spain Sings: Fifty Loyalist Ballads Adapted by American Poets,* edited by Rolfe Humphries and M. J. Benardete. The poems were chosen by Benardete from the first four issues of the weekly *El Mono Azul,* published by the Alianza de Intelectuales Antifascistas para la Defensa de la Cultura. Two pages of ballads under the title "Romancero de la Guerra Civil" appeared in each issue. Humphries wrote in the foreword that the poets who answered the call to adapt the ballads to English verse had worked from rough translations but also with the Spanish originals. In her copy of the book, Porter wrote in the margin: "Not true—for me, at least. I worked *only* from Spanish. K. A. P."[83] In a brief introduction, Lorenza Varela made a distinction between the *romancero* poets and "the mock popular poets," who "stuff . . . their books with elegies and sentimental trash, aimed at arousing the worst human sentiments." Varela says that people and poet have collaborated in the *romancero* of the present civil war, a collaboration "traditionally necessary for the flowering of epic poetry." Even if Porter could not wholeheartedly approve of art that had a political end, she no doubt approved of the source of this poetry, as she would have approved of the symbolism in the poem she translated.[84] The olive grove was itself a symbol of Spanish culture and the Spanish people.

After 1937 Porter wrote fewer poems, having completed "Old Mortality" at the end of 1936, she finished "Pale Horse, Pale Rider" in 1938 and "The Leaning Tower" in 1940, and she began earnestly trying to finish *Ship of Fools*. During one of her many hiatuses from the novel, she wrote the bawdy little "Morning Song of the Tinker's Bitch"[85] and may also have written "afternoon walk to her," an undated, whimsical poem ostensibly about California and her own wild travels back and forth across the country as she tried to stay financially afloat with contracts at film studios, lecture tours, and teaching appointments at universities. The title "afternoon walk to her"— with no capital letter and a truncated meaning ("her" is an adjective modifying an elided noun that would identify "her" destination)—establishes the incompleteness of the persona's "pilgrimage." Within the poem, there are no real stops, only an accumulation of impressions and thoughts as the "me" hurries on her way. Without the nominative "I" and only the objective "me," there is double vision. In the reflexiveness of the viewpoint Porter is stepping outside herself, watching her own frenetic movements in a social context that is unsympathetic and threatening. There are, however, fleeting "songs in the air" and "infusions of wonder" that transform "clay." In other words, there is the capacity to be awed and to imagine that lifts life beyond the material and the mundane, a theme obliquely addressed in "Enchanted." The living plants, trees, shrubs, and flowers, flanking the walker on her "wood-edged way" represent the natural world that opposes the "alchemists . . . / . . . blinding me." The overall impression is that of a stream of consciousness, to which modern free verse had an affinity. Porter may have acquired the techniques apparent in this poem from some of the traditional poets she knew, but more likely she learned such free-verse techniques from modern poets such as Pound, Eliot, Verlaine, and Rimbaud.

The last poem Porter published was "After a Long Journey," an expansion of "Bouquet for October." In 1957 she offered it to Russell Lynes for *Harper's.* The theme and tone of the later poem had been established in 1931 when it was the embryonic "Bouquet for October," and Porter's changes do not so much reflect her late direction in poetry as they amplify and make specific certain vague references in the 1931 poem. Porter added appositives, adjectives, and adjective phrases; extended catalogues; and illustrated certain assertions with examples. As Porter wrote the poem in 1931, she seemed to be warning Pressly that their love was out of season. In the 1957 version of it she is looking back sadly to the period that was a prologue to a marriage that was not destined to last.

The images and scenes in the poem are those of the crossing to Bremerhaven on the German ship *Werra* and of the few months spent in Germany after the landing. After they left Germany, Porter and Pressly spent much of the years between 1932 and 1936 in Paris, a place where they found some shared contentment, but it is not Paris that is the focus of the poem. Germany and early winter symbolized for Porter the failure of love, and that was the subject of both versions of the poem. There is another reason that Porter in 1957 did not go beyond the voyage and the months in Germany as she expanded the poem. She was in the last stages of completing *Ship of Fools,* and her characters Jenny Brown and David Scott are the fictional counterparts to the 1931 Porter and Pressly. There are, in fact, added phrases and words in the 1957 poem that have direct bearing on the novel.

In "Bouquet for October" Porter had proposed the memory of sun as a consolation for the frost of October. In "After a Long Journey," she specifically names Mexico as the home of the sun and amplifies it with images of "mangos and melons / And the feathery shade of the Peruano tree in our eyes." The beginning of *Ship of Fools* is set in Mexico, and Jenny remembers her and David's time in that country with nostalgia. The sixth stanza of "After a Long Journey" picks up the catalogue of events from the third stanza of "Bouquet for October" and becomes more specifically personal to Porter's and Pressly's voyage. Porter made the "cold shudder of ships" into "the loud cold shudders of our ship that sailed on sea and meadow / The Caribbean, the Atlantic, the river Weser" and added to "the spouting of whales" and the visage of "friars" references to "Santa Cruz de Tenerife, or the slender girls with doll hats tied to their foreheads, / And water jars on their heads running wildly sure-footed as deer / In the steep stony pathways. . . ." The scene is used twice in *Ship of Fools,* once in language similar to that of the poem and a second time in the self-revelatory words of William Denny. First, David, an artist, views the scene:

A young slender girl, limber and tough as a ballet dancer, in a short tight black dress showing her bare brown legs, her head swathed in a small square black shawl with a tiny hat no larger than a doll's resting on her forehead, secured somehow under the knot of her covered hair, hurled herself across their path and leaped up the rocky incline ahead of them, turning sharply to the left on a narrower path, sure-footed as a deer and as wild. On her head she carried a great flat tray loaded with battered metal water cans, and under this weight, in her worn tennis shoes, she went at flying speed uphill, in a half-run with rigid shoulders, raised chin and extravagantly swaying hips, her arms spread like wings. (377)

Denny, in contrast, describes the girls in vulgar terms: "You know those girls with water cans on their heads? Well, one of them give me the eye . . .—so I took out after her, . . . and honest to God, she went stomping up and down those rocky ridges and paths like a mountain goat . . ." (380). The difference between the deer of the poem's idealized scene and Denny's mountain goat simile defines his own "goatishness." The artistry in both the poem and the novel is brought into relief when the two imaginative passages are measured against Porter's more nearly objective description of the "milk-women" in her letter to Caroline Gordon: "And the milk-women in their short black dresses, bare legs, their heads swathed in a black shawl with a little round hat, secured in the back by an elastic under their knot of hair, carrying great flat trays loaded with battered milk cans. They have a charming walk, half-run, with rigid head and shoulders and wildly swaying hips. . . ."[86]

An entire stanza Porter added to the poem encapsulates a major theme of the novel. In the poem the persona asks, "Shall we ever forget how once we traveled to a far country, / A strange land, ourselves strangers to all and to each other?" She comments, "The morning country of love and we two still strangers—." In the novel's opening frame, the embarking passengers, nameless at this point in the narrative, are strangers to one another, suspicious and hostile. They grudgingly become acquainted, in a way, during the voyage. But when the ship sails into port at Bremen and the passengers line up for disembarking, "Eyes met eyes again vaguely, almost without recognition and no further speech. They were becoming strangers again . . ." (494).

After Porter completed *Ship of Fools,* she wrote very little poetry, and none seriously. Reverting to her early love of medieval and Renaissance lyrics, she occasionally composed Christmas or Valentine "songs" that she would send to selected friends. Such were her last known efforts to produce poetry.

The fifty-one poems in this collection—presented chronologically according to Porter's writing of first drafts, as nearly as such dates can be determined—reveal considerable detail about her art. They reflect in large measure the subjects and themes of particular fictional works that Porter developed concurrently with the poetry, and they illustrate the degree to which she blended an older literature into a modernist aesthetic. Her gradual movement into modernism was precipitated by the influence of poets whose work she admired. Her entrenchment in the movement was encouraged by the influence of poets with whom she became friends.

When Porter reviewed the *Letters of Ezra Pound: 1907–1941,* she recounted a conversation she had had with Hart Crane in 1930. She and Crane had been reading again *Pavannes and Divisions,* when Crane reacted to one of Pound's dogmatic statements and exclaimed: "I'm tired of Ezra Pound!" Porter had asked him, "Well, who else is there?" Crane then agreed that "there's nobody like him, nobody to take his place." Porter concludes, "This was the truth for us then, and it is still the truth for many of us who came up, were educated, you might say, in contemporary literature, not at schools at all but by five writers: Henry James, James Joyce, W. B. Yeats, T. S. Eliot, and Ezra Pound."[87]

Ezra Pound was indeed an important early influence on Porter. She said she was aware of Pound's translations when they first began appearing in 1915, about the same time that she discovered Yeats. Soon afterward she became acquainted with Pound's original poetry. In 1954 she wrote an admiring letter to Pound from Liège, Belgium, where she had gone on a Fulbright appointment. She began her letter "Dear Ezra" and told him, "I presume to call you thus on the grounds of our entirely one-sided friendship getting on for forty years." She told him that during her public poetry readings, she often read his "The Cloak," "The River Merchant's Wife," "Song of the Bowmen of Shu," "The Jewel Stairs Grievance," and "A Ballad of the Mulberry Road."[88]

In spite of Porter's discovery of Pound in the same year she discovered Yeats, there is no doubt that Yeats was the more important early influence on Porter's poetry. She identified Yeats as the first of the moderns she read,[89] and there are particular aspects of his poetry and philosophy that are broadly reflected in Porter's own art and philosophy. Yeats was a transitional influence on Porter because his lyrics would have appealed to her before she gravitated toward modernism. When she moved toward the new current, she found that stream in Yeats also.

The influence of T. S. Eliot on Porter was similar to that of Pound. Eliot was for Porter the consummate craftsman, the modernist with whom she shared a reverence for the classics as a point of departure for the modern age. Although she contended that when Eliot embraced religion his poetic powers failed, she consistently praised his poetry. She wrote to Glenway Wescott in 1940, "I admire Eliot tremendously, but not in the role of curé of souls, Church of England Style."[90] It was probably through Porter's reading of Eliot's poetry that she first became explicitly aware of the symbolist poets, from Baudelaire through Mallarmé to Valéry and Rilke.[91] Her affinity with the symbolist aesthetic, first intuited by her in the poetry of Poe, Blake, and Yeats, would have been further strengthened by her friendship with poets and new critics Allen Tate and Robert Penn Warren in the 1920s and with Cleanth Brooks in the

1930s. The symbolists' emphasis on musicality appealed to Porter's own identification of poetry and music. If she explained the symbolism in her fiction as unconscious on her part,[92] she would acknowledge a degree of calculation in the poetry. She was not so far distanced from Eliot as one would think when he later rejected some of the extreme premises of the symbolist movement (in *From Poe to Valéry*). She herself would take a stand on clarity and on the commonality of symbols.[93]

In naming poets she admired or those she disdained (there was little middle ground), Porter was quite clear. But beyond general assessment, discussing poets' personal philosophies, or describing the overall effect of poems, Porter was uncomfortable explaining her critical positions. She told Allen Tate in 1931, "I want to write about your poems, but you know that I can't say anything further than I like this, or I prefer this, the reasons I give wouldn't mean much."[94] Porter took a Tate volume along on her voyage to Europe later in the year and said to Caroline Gordon, Tate's wife, "Substance, and 'tone' that mysterious and indispensable quality he attributes to the work of Ezra Pound also belong even more to his own."[95] Still later she explained to Gordon and Tate why she did not review Tate's *Pope*: "After long pondering and holding of the head and beating of the brow, I decided that I know nothing about poetry and it would be presumptious [*sic*] of me to try to give an opinion."[96] She wrote to Robert Penn Warren in 1957, "Your new poems *Promises* have given me joy and pleasure, and I would hardly know how to say whether this poem or that was lovelier than another. (Maybe that's a soft word for such as Ballad of a Sweet Dream of Peace, which not only chilled my blood and raised my hair, but damned near tore the latter out entirely."[97]

If Porter was unable to discuss technical aspects of poetry or unwilling to venture into the area of formal literary criticism, she was comfortable in discussing ideas in poems and in

51

indulging her love of poetry. In letters or autobiographical notes, Porter discussed Goethe, Dante, Catullus, Höderlin, Villon, Baudelaire, Valéry, Rilke, and others, often in terms of their broad philosophies or their general contributions to art. Sometimes she discussed their personal lives as evidence of their artistic commitment (or lack thereof).[98] She also enjoyed merry games of writing poetry with friends. She composed doggerel with Josephine Herbst and John Hermann, quoted favorite poems with Robert Penn Warren, and won a party prize at the home of Ford Madox Ford for writing a sonnet in ten minutes.[99] When Porter began to give readings of her work in the 1930s, she would occasionally read selections from other people's poetry—a practice that perhaps stemmed from her youthful performing of ballads on the Lyceum circuit.[100] These occasional interspersements progressed to entire presentations of poetry. In her stints as a university faculty member, she commonly taught courses in poetry, describing her intention to make students acquainted with poetry as a first step toward making them like it. She told Warren that for her poetry course at the University of Michigan, she "settled on the lyric as the thing" and jumped her students back to Catullus and Petronius Arbiter, took them "on a roller coaster ride through the medieval Latin poets straight into late middle English—well, a couple of the snappier things of Chaucer's to Lydgate—my what a long stretch there, and what a fall—Skelton, and then the Elizabethans, Seventeenth century, Eighteenth, Nineteen, and so, in no time with their hair in their teeth and a roaring in their ears, we are soon fetching up in the beautiful hurly-burly of our times."[101]

Porter's fondness for the lyric had not wavered, and since 1952, she had been trying to put together an anthology for Bantam Books. She planned to call her book "Katherine Anne Porter's Favorite Lyric Poems" or "The Light of the World," after Joubert. She also planned to organize the poems by century in much the same way she organized her class at the University of Michigan. In her correspondence with Grace Bechtold, associate editor at Bantam Books, Porter outlined the plan of the anthology. She tells Bechtold that the poems are being chosen "to illustrate the development and changes in . . . the lyric in the English language" and that "the really important key sections" of the collection are "yet to come": "the very early Latin, and the early Christian Latin, which are the most important because they are the key to all that follow"; Porter insists on having the authority to determine which poems will be included (2 September 1955, McKeldin). Although her proposed table of contents is incomplete, it provides a glimpse of the breadth of her knowledge of poetry and the range of her admiration.[102]

Katherine Anne Porter's own poetry evolved from her love of music and performance as well as from the traditional poetry on which she had been nurtured. From "A Dying Child" to "After a Long Journey," her poems reveal an effort to give expression and form to her deeply felt personal experiences. If her fiction objectifies those experiences more eloquently, the poetry allows us to trace on another plane her artistic development, and it occasionally charms us in the process.

Notes

1. Porter told David Locher in the 1950s that she had written more than 200 poems (author's telephone interview with David Locher, 11 December 1994). Porter told Allen Tate and Caroline Gordon in a letter of 6 March 1932 that she had "rummaged through and through all the two hundred fragments of poems which testify to my grim determination to write a poem or die" to find one she could send to them. See *Letters of Katherine Anne Porter,* ed. Isabel Bayley (New York: Atlantic Monthly Press, 1990), 72.

2. Porter mentioned her youthful introduction to poetry many times. See, for example, Barbara Thompson, "Katherine Anne Porter: An Interview," *Paris Review* 8 (Winter–Spring 1963): 87–114; reprinted in *Katherine Anne Porter: Conversations,* ed. Joan Givner (Jackson: University of Mississippi Press, 1987).

3. Porter wrote to her nephew Paul Porter, "It is true I see and hear my people and my episodes rather than think them; well, it is all thought, naturally, but with me the words do come last . . . (19 July 1949, Paul Porter Papers). See also Thompson, "Katherine Anne Porter: An Interview."

4. Although the general biographical information about Porter I cite is available in the standard sources and in the Porter Papers at the University of Maryland, Joan Givner is credited especially with uncovering important facts about Porter's year at the Thomas School, her first marriage, and her years in Texas and Colorado between 1912 and 1919. Porter's time in Mexico has been detailed carefully by Thomas Walsh.

5. "The Old Order" was the first title of Porter's piece "The Journey." She changed the title when she appropriated "The Old Order" for the encompassing title of seven short pieces that constitute a short novel.

6. See Thomas F. Walsh, *Katherine Anne Porter and Mexico: The Illusion of Eden* (Austin: University of Texas Press, 1992).

7. See William McGuire, *Poetry's Catbird Seat: The Consultantship in Poetry in the English Language at the Library of Congress, 1937–1987* (Washington: Library of Congress, 1988).

8. Although Porter dated the finished manuscript of *Ship of Fools* "Yaddo, August 1941 / Pigeon Cove, August, 1961" and frequently commented that the novel began as a log she kept on a 1931 voyage, there is considerable evidence that a vague idea Porter had for a novel during the late 1920s was a loosely embryonic version of *Ship of Fools,* a three-part work that was to conclude with events set in "the present scene" and to focus on "the sick and crumbling society with some of the cures offered by diverse Saviours. . . . The various roads by which characters separate and go to their several ends . . ." (Notes, McKeldin).

The other two parts of the planned novel dropped off in the early 1930s as short stories in the Miranda cycle and as "Noon Wine."

9. For a list of journalistic pieces, see Kathryn Hilt and Ruth M. Alvarez, *Katherine Anne Porter: An Annotated Bibliography* (New York: Garland, 1990), 79–103. The poem is "Texas: By the Gulf of Mexico." The fables include "The Shattered Star," "The Faithful Princess," "The Magic Ear Ring," and "The Adventures of Hadji." See also Porter's *My Chinese Marriage* and *Outline of Mexican Popular Arts and Crafts*.

10. Porter as vice president of the National Institute of Arts and Letters (1950–1952) was only the second woman to hold the post.

11. Undated notes, McKeldin.

12. Undated notes on "Privacy," McKeldin.

13. KAP to L. Tacheechee, 29 November 1929, McKeldin. See also Enrique Hank Lopez, *Conversations with Katherine Anne Porter: Refugee from Indian Creek* (Boston: Little, Brown, 1981), 42.

14. See "Preface to the Revised Edition," Joan Givner, *Katherine Anne Porter: A Life* (Athens: University of Georgia Press, 1992), 1.

15. Undated notes, McKeldin. See also KAP to Gertrude Beitel, 7 August 1957, McKeldin.

16. KAP to family ("Dear Darlings"), 20 December 1920, McKeldin. In the letter Porter told Gay she wrote the poem the first day she arrived in Mexico, 5 November, but on another manuscript copy of the poem Porter wrote "New York 1920."

17. KAP to Gertrude Beitel, 7 August 1957, McKeldin.

18. Porter wrote to Robert Penn Warren, "Let me tell you something about poetry which will probably explain something. I read it first when I was about ten, and I cannot even think of it now without a rising of the hair: 'Fear no more the heat of the sun . . .' remember that?" (27 February 1947, *Letters*, 132).

19. Porter's interest in Blake ran deep. She wrote to Albert Erskine about Foster Damon's study of Blake: "I love that apocalyptic world in which the man lived, who saw flights of angels when

he walked beside the sea. . . . The great mystics outwear all other company, I suppose for their very lack of horizons" (2 February 1938, McKeldin). In 1944 and 1945 she was trying to write an essay on Blake (notes for unfinished piece, McKeldin).

20. See "Striking the Lyric Note in Mexico," "The New Man and the New Order," "Xochimilco," "The Mexican Trinity," "Where Presidents Have No Friends," and "Two Ancient Mexican Pyramids—the Core of a City Unknown Until a Few Years Ago."

21. Transcription of 1971 Interview with Porter, McKeldin.

22. See "Love and Hate" and "Letters to a Nephew: Observations on—Pets, Poets, Sex, Love, Hate, Fame, Treason."

23. See Walsh, 64.

24. Glenway Wescott points out Porter's womb/tomb symbolism in her fiction. See "Katherine Anne Porter Personally," in *Images of Truth* (New York: Harper and Row, 1962), 25–58.

25. Notes for a foreword to a planned anthology of short stories, McKeldin.

26. "Ay, Que Chamaco."

27. In undated notes at McKeldin, Porter accused De la Selva of seducing the sister of one of Rivera's models and wrote, "If Salomon met the Virgin Mary, he would introduce himself as the Holy Ghost."

28. KAP to Delafield Day, 17 July 1928, Papers of Delafield Day Spier, McKeldin.

29. Notes, McKeldin.

30. Notes, McKeldin. Millay's poem appeared in *Second April* in 1921; the parodied stanza is the following:

> Down, you mongrel, Death!
>   Back into your kennel!
> I have stolen breath
>   In a stalk of fennel!
> You shall scratch and you shall whine
>   Many a night, and you shall worry
>   Many a bone, before you bury
> One sweet bone of mine!

31. "The Poet and Her Imp."
32. This poem exists among Porter's notes at McKeldin with a variation that replaces Sandburg's name with that of Christopher Morley.
33. See Walsh, 120 and 238 n. 30. Porter planned to write a long essay about Sor Juana and Mistral (notes for "Two Spanish American Poets," McKeldin) and briefly considered translating Amado Nervo's *Life of Sor Juana* (KAP to Donald Elder, 6 March 1941, *Letters*, 198).
34. See "The Situation in American Writing: Seven Questions."
35. Pound's *Cathay* appeared in 1915.
36. See Walsh, 93.
37. See KAP to Rolfe Humphries, n.d. [1924], and KAP to Genevieve Taggard, 3 April 1924, Taggard Papers, New York Public Library, New York, N.Y. Porter said the original title of "Requiescat—" was "Last Choice."
38. An account of this walking tour is among Porter's notes at McKeldin.
39. See Walsh, 95. In manuscript Porter called the poem "Feast of Santiago."
40. Porter had an unusually strong interest in Baudelaire. At the time of her death, she owned many books about Baudelaire as well as collections of his works in both French and English. Marginalia in the volumes indicate that Porter read his works in French. Porter also had substantial notes on Rimbaud, whom she discussed with Morton Zabel, among others.
41. Notes, McKeldin.
42. Porter mentions that there are four witch poems but also suggests that she may have drafted one or more of them in 1922. KAP to Genevieve Taggard, 3 April [1924], Taggard Papers.
43. See Walsh, 83–88, 98, 129, 155.
44. Mary Doherty, Porter's friend in Mexico and the model for Laura in "Flowering Judas," told Walsh that Porter had an abortion during the De la Selva affair (see Walsh, 64).
45. In her letter of 3 April to Genevieve Taggard, Porter says the

poems were written in Mexico two years ago this month. Porter was in Mexico in April of 1922 but not April of 1923. The year of the 3 April letter therefore would have to be 1924.

46. Porter says that "Ordeal by Invocation" is one of the four witch poems. KAP to Genevieve Taggard, 3 April [1924], Taggard Papers, New York Public Library. Porter also mentions another poem she calls "Causerie II," which may be a fourth, as yet undiscovered, witch poem.

47. See "Live Memories of a Growing Season."

48. Notes, McKeldin.

49. See Walsh, 95–96.

50. In "Letter to a Spaniard" [Aguilera], n.d., McKeldin.

51. KAP to Genevieve Taggard, 3 April [1924], Taggard Archives.

52. KAP to Russell Lynes, 10 August 1955, Russell Lynes Collection, Beinecke.

53. Givner, *Life*, 172–75.

54. KAP to Josephine Herbst, 5 May 1928, Josephine Herbst Collection, Beinecke.

55. See Jane DeMouy, *Katherine Anne Porter's Women: The Eye of Her Fiction* (Austin: University of Texas Press, 1983), 61–72.

56. The variation on the sonnet was especially evident in Wyatt's poetry.

57. In her copy of a Dickinson volume at McKeldin, Porter noted that De la Selva read every poem to her (in Mexico in 1921–1922).

58. Manuscript at McKeldin.

59. KAP to Josephine Herbst, 21 May 1929, Beinecke. Porter possibly experienced a real hurricane in Bermuda; she describes such a storm in a letter to Josephson of 29 April 1929, Beinecke.

60. KAP to Eugene Pressly, n.d. [1931], McKeldin.

61. KAP to Eugene Pressly, n.d. [1931], McKeldin.

62. Porter had a habit of recycling titles. "The Fig Tree" was also a title for an early (pre-1929) draft of "Holiday."

63. See "Old Gods and New Messiahs" and "These Pictures Must Be Seen."

64. See "Leaving the Petate" and "Example to the Young."
65. See KAP to Paul O'Higgins, Winter 1931, *Letters,* 66–67.
66. Monroe Wheeler to KAP, 3 March 1932, McKeldin.
67. KAP to Barbara Harrison, 17 March 1932, *Letters,* 79–80.
68. Willard Trask may be the person Wheeler found. In her acknowledgements Porter thanks him for his help.
69. KAP to Monroe Wheeler, 22 November 1933, *Letters,* 99–100.
70. KAP to Monroe Wheeler and Glenway Wescott, 9 August 1934, *Letters,* 110–11. Porter also sent the poem and her translation to Josephine Herbst. Inscribed manuscript in the John Hermann Collection at the Harry Ransom Humanities Research Center, University of Texas at Austin.
71. Consider "They that go down to the sea in ships, that do business in great waters, these see the works of the Lord, and his wonders in the deep" from Psalm 107 (23–24), King James version; "Lhude sing cuccu!" from "Sumer is icumen in" (anonymous, ca. 1250); "The world is grown so bad, / That wrens make prey where eagles dare not perch" from *King Richard III* 1.3.70–71; and "Thy wish was father, Harry, to that thought" from *King Henry IV, Part II,* 4.5.92.
72. The odd number of stanzas (eleven) suggests the incompleteness or the continuation of the pattern. The first ten stanzas alternate patterns of rhyme. The first stanza is characterized by identical rhyme, a version of *rime riche,* in the first three lines. The fourth line is different and therefore emphasized because it breaks the pattern. The second stanza is constructed on the pattern of alternating rhyme, *abab* (although in the second stanza the a rhyme is a near-rhyme). Stanzas three through ten repeat the alternating pattern established by the first two stanzas. The last stanza breaks the pattern with an *abcb* rhyme. There is also a calculated use of syllabic lineation in the poem. No two stanzas are alike in terms of number of syllables in their sequential lines, an illustration of a uniqueness that is subsumed by the larger pattern of the poem's rhyme.
73. Notes, McKeldin.

74. Notes, McKeldin.
75. See Kenneth Burke, "Four Master Tropes," in *A Grammar of Motives* (Berkeley: University of California Press, 1969). Porter had sent "Bouquet for October" to Kenneth Burke to place wherever he thought appropriate.
76. Notes, McKeldin. Porter probably meant that she had not gone to the grave for many years, or not in her adult life. She is likely to have been taken to the cemetery during her childhood.
77. Notes, McKeldin.
78. See Edward G. Schwartz, "The Fictions of Memory," *Southwest Review* 45 (Summer 1960): 204–15.
79. Paul Porter, Porter's nephew, in talks at the Katherine Anne Porter Centennial celebration at College Park in 1991 and at the library in Kyle, Texas, 15 May 1995, has commented on his aunt's gardening skills and love of roses.
80. KAP to Rolfe Humphries, n.d., McKeldin.
81. Rolfe Humphries to KAP, 9 June 1937, McKeldin.
82. Rolfe Humphries to KAP (telegram), 17 June 1937, McKeldin.
83. Porter's copy, McKeldin.
84. See Porter's "The Mexican Trinity," *Freeman* 3 (3 August 1921): 493–95; reprinted, slightly revised, in *Collected Essays*.
85. The manuscript of this poem is in the possession of the author. Porter sent the poem to Russell Lynes with the following marginal comment: "Written after listening to Dyer-Bennett, Burl Ives, et al, bragging to lute and guitar, by Katherine Anne Porter, bragging 3 July 1946."
86. *Letters,* 54–55.
87. "Yours, Ezra Pound."
88. KAP to Ezra Pound, 22 October 1954, Beinecke.
89. Porter, "From the Notebooks of Katherine Anne Porter—Yeats, Joyce, Eliot, Pound," *Southern Review,* n.s., 1 (Summer 1965): 570–73.
90. See KAP to Glenway Wescott, 14 June 1940, *Letters,* 180–81, and KAP to Paul Porter (nephew), 21 May 1943, *Letters,* 263. See also Porter's "Notes on a Criticism of Thomas Hardy" and "On First Meeting T. S. Eliot." On the opening day of her class at Stanford (5 January 1949), Porter taught Eliot and Valéry.

91. Porter was well acquainted with the works of Rilke as well as Baudelaire and Valéry. See "Rilke and Benvenuto." See also KAP to Babette Deutsch, 30 December 1941, *Letters*, 216–17; KAP to Paul Porter (nephew), 19 November 1942, *Letters*, 252; and KAP to Albert Erskine, 19 August 1940 and 26 August 1940, McKeldin.

92. See *Recent Southern Fiction: A Panel Discussion* (Macon, Ga.: Wesleyan College, 1961).

93. KAP to Paul Porter, 28 October 1954, *Letters*, 464–65.

94. KAP to Allen Tate, 27 January 1931, *Letters*, 27–30.

95. KAP to Caroline Gordon, 28 August 1931, *Letters*, 57.

96. KAP to Carolina Gordon and Allen Tate, 6 March 1932, *Letters*, 72.

97. KAP to Robert Penn Warren, 26 September 1957, Beinecke.

98. See, e.g., KAP to William Harlan Hale, 8 July 1932, McKeldin. Porter disliked Stephen Spender and Konstantinos Kavafis on personal grounds (notes, McKeldin).

99. See KAP to Paul Porter (brother), 8 March 1932, *Letters*, 78; KAP to Andrew Lytle, 30 August 1953, *Letters*, 442; and the note about doggerel verse in Josephine Herbst's photograph album in the John Hermann Collection at the Harry Ransom Humanities Research Center at the University of Texas at Austin.

100. See "Poetry of Our Times," *Variety*, 29 April 1953, 39.

101. KAP to Robert Penn Warren, 16 October 1953, *Letters*, 452.

102. Notes, McKeldin. Aside from anonymous medieval lyrics and translations of ancient Greek and Latin poems, Porter intended to include selections from the works of the following poets: Leonie Adams, W. H. Auden, John Betjeman, Elizabeth Bishop, John Peale Bishop, Louis Bogan, John Malcolm Brinnin, Emily Brontë, Hart Crane, E. E. Cummings, J. V. Cunningham, Emily Dickinson, John Dryden, T. S. Eliot, Dudley Fitts, Robert Fitzgerald, Robin Flower, Robert Frost, Oliver St. John Gogarty, Robert Graves, Thomas Hardy, Norman Harris, Anthony Hecht, George Herbert, F. R. Higgins, G. M. Hopkins, A. E. Housman, Barbara Howe, Mildren Howland, Randall Jarrell, James Joyce, D. H. Lawrence, Robert Lowell, Archibald MacLeish, Herman

Melville, W. S. Merwin, Marianne Moore, Howard Moss, Ogden Nash, Edgar Allan Poe, Ezra Pound, John Crowe Ransom, Edwin Arlington Robinson, Theodore Roethke, Christina Rossetti, James Schulyer, Edith Sitwell, Sacheverall Sitwell, William Jay Smith, Theodore Spencer, Wallace Stevens, Allen Tate, Dylan Thomas, Helen Waddell, Robert Penn Warren, Walt Whitman, William Carlos Williams, Yvor Winters, and W. B. Yeats.

Katherine Anne Porter in Corpus Christi, Texas, 1912, when she wrote and published "Texas: By the Gulf of Mexico."

Katherine Anne Porter, New York City, Winter 1919–1920, when she drafted "A Dying Child."

Salomón de la Selva, Nicaraguan poet with whom Porter had an affair in Mexico in the early 1920s.

mexico 1923

Katherine Anne Porter wearing China Poblana, Mexican costume, Cuernavaca, 1923.

Francis Aguilera, 1923–1924. Porter had a love affair with him.

Katherine Anne Porter in Bermuda 1929. She wrote "Night Blooming Cereus" and "West Indian Island" here.

Hart Crane in Porter's garden in Mixcoac, 1931.

Eugene Pressly aboard the *Werra* in 1931. Porter's journey from Veracruz to Bremerhaven with him inspired "Bouquet for October." The journey and their subsequent failed marriage inspired "After a Long Journey."

Katherine Anne Porter in Paris, 1933.

Barbara Harrison and Monroe Wheeler in Davos, Switzerland, 1934. They published *Katherine Anne Porter's French Song-Book* in 1933.

Mary Alice Jones Porter, Katherine Anne Porter's mother, ca. 1885.

Mary Alice Jones Porter's grave at Indian Creek cemetery.

Katherine Anne Porter on stroll in 1940s, Santa Monica, California.

Katherine Anne Porter at Congress of Cultural Freedom, Paris, 1952. Last row, second from left is Stephen Spender. Front row, third from left, James T. Farrell; fourth from left, Robert Lowell; fifth from left, Glenway Wescott; and sixth from left, Porter. At table, left to right, André Malraux, Jules Supervielle, Denis de Rougemont, William Faulkner, and W. H. Auden.

Katherine Anne Porter in 1954 at the University of Michigan, where she taught a course in poetry.

Katherine Anne Porter with unidentified man and Father Raymond Roseliep at a poetry reading in Georgetown, 7 August 1964.

The Poems

Texas: By the Gulf of Mexico

Ye shivering ones of the frozen North, list to my happy song
    Of the seventh heaven nestled here below,
In our rich, fertile valleys, midst sunkissed fruits and flowers
    In Texas, by the Gulf of Mexico.

For here, lieth without measure, peaceful rest and gold enstore;
    So to quiet the vague longing of your mind,
Come build yourself a cottage, plant roses by the door,
    Then forget the sleet and snow you left behind.

For the man who knows his business—yea, the man who's
    wondrous wise—
    Knows that Texas is a paradise. I trow,
Far better than a palace 'neath the frozen northern skies
    Is an orange grove around a bungalow.

In all this song and flight of bird beneath skies of clearest blue
    Above the fluttering jessamine trees that sway
To every wanton breeze that waft their fragrance sweet to you,
    You'll find a fresh delight for each new day.

But there's other things as perfect as this ever changing scene,
    Where homes spring up as flowers on a hill—
For your garden grows on gaily through the winter, fresh and green,
    Bringing bright and jingling coins into your till.

So, lock the door and call the dog, and catch the nearest train
    That departs to where the sunset's golden glow
Is a forecast of the money you will seek, and not in vain—
    In Texas, by the Gulf of Mexico.

published in *Gulf Coast Citrus Fruit Grower
and Southern Nurseryman*, 1912

A Dying Child

It is too quiet now in this house where you lay
Watching the latticed window vines swaying in the summer
    sun—
Saying O dearly dearly I love the light of this day,
And all the living things that flower or run.

It is too quiet now at windows and on the stairs
And never again will you lift up your hands and say
O dearly dearly I love the dress the summer garden wears
And dearly dearly I love the light of day.

written 1920, revised 1957,
unpublished

Song with Castanet Accompaniment

"He knew the anguish of the marrow,
The ague of the skeleton."

T. S. Eliot

"The clean bones crying in the flesh."

Elinor Wylie

"'Tis that every mother's son,
Travails with a skeleton."

A. E. Housman

When she peered in the looking-glass
A jocund skull regarded her;
Neat bones stared palely through a skin
Sleekened with oil, tainted with myrrh.

She smoothed her cheeks and left them rose,
She touched her lips and made them red:
"And I shall rattle like shaken dice
When Gabriel drags me out of bed!

My ribs shall chatter like housewife's keys,
Dry joints bend at the shuttered gate,
Eyeless to gaze through a chink in the wall,
At the limitless impudence of fate:

Who weaponed me with melting flesh
To war with potent rain and sun——
And strips me before the ultimate Eye,
An apologetic skeleton!"

written ca. 1921–1922, unpublished

[Down, you Mongrel Death]

Down, you mongrel Death, back, you mangy swindle
E'er my light shall fade, the sun itself shall dwindle!
E'er my voice shall cease, Time itself will dry up,
While in the antic hay my lad and I shall lie up.

Back, you mongrel Death, down, you dingy nuisance!
With your talk of manners, custom, and good usance—
I thumb my nose at you and them and eke at Good Society,
Leave me with my gay glad love and natural impropriety!
   Down, you mongrel Death, back into your kennel,
   Leave me flat upon my back among the rue and fennel.

dated 1922 by Porter, unpublished

Variation 1001: To the Foolish Virgins
Who Aren't Gathering Roses

Ladies why idle you there
Wasting the cool of the morning?
I've come to sing you a song
And bring you a warning.

Let me sell you a rhyme
For a bright penny—
Now is a better time
To love, than any!

Loving is not for long
The bright day is flying—
Ladies, there's only a breath
Between living and dying!

initialed by Porter and dated as
Mexico City, Spring 1922; unpublished

Ordeal by Ploughshare

There was also a dream
I did not tell:
The wind-blown clangour
Of an old bell:

A thin changeling creature
Babbling her prayers;
Blood-coloured torchlight
Drenching the stairs.

It was dead of the night
And a black sky—
No friendly star
To watch her die.

A harsh bitter crying
But no clear word,
Solemn deep singing—
These things I heard:

A tittering fountain
In a gold shell,
And the long screaming
Of the mad bell.

The lost changeling creature
Stared, and stumbled
On the white ploughshares:
The dream crumbled—

All the dark multitude
Vanished, and after
There trailed a whirlwind
Of ghostly laughter!

This is the dream
I weep to tell
When I hear the crying
Of an old bell.

written ca. 1922–1923, unpublished

This Transfusion

You need not be afraid, I shall not wound
Your pride with my edged scorn,
Nor flagellate with my despairs
The surface of your heart:
For this my hate
Is not a lash, nor thorn
But a measureless, distilled
Vial of torment endlessly refilled.
And it shall fix upon your senses so,
Shall of your slakeless fibres be such part
As your wild blood shall mix within your veins
My hard, enduring pains,
Incorporate with your immediate being.
And if your pulse should quicken, it shall be
To the sole desire of death, the ease of hell,
From this transfusion that was the life of me.

written ca. 1922–1923, unpublished

Witch's Song

Tie my left great toe to my slim right thumb,
Tie my left slim thumb to my right great toe—
Let your scared green faces be smitten dumb,
When the water shall cradle me so.

The water will bear me, I shall float,
The waves will make me a little boat,
The winds will blow and I shall have breath—
Death by drowning is not my death!

The wind shall blow and I shall have breath,
Death by drowning is not my death!

The lake is my friend—a witch and the water
Are bound with a tie—are mother and daughter;
But the Fire is my lover, and licks my bones
And the roar of his joy it covers my groans.
  My mother the Water,
  My lover the Fire
  One shall deliver me
  One shall betray me
  For an old hire.
  Both shall surrender me
  Grieving give over me
  Unto my Lord, unto my sovereign
  Death!

Tie my left great toe to my slim right thumb,
Tie my left slim thumb to my right great toe—
Let your scared green faces be smitten dumb,
When the water shall cradle me so!

written ca. 1922–1923, unpublished.

Enchanted

On these familiar stones, this homely stair,
I set my feet as I am used to do;
I draw the curtains in my quiet house,
And feel the winds blow through.

Oh, tranquil roofs and muted drowsing bells,
Full of old secrets, marvel and be still
To see a wraith of fiery magic pass
Over my dark door sill.

Do not bewilder me, swift hunting moon,
With arrows of amazement in my eyes;
If these steep roofs should bloom, these stones should sing,
I would not know surprise!

written 1922–1923, published in
the *York Evening Post*, August 1923

Three Songs from Mexico

I
In Tepozotlan

I should like to see again
That honey-colored girl
Dipping her arms shoulder-deep
In the hives of honey.
Who can tell me where she is gone,
That untroubled innocent
Whose hands were kissed by bees,
And whose fingers dripped honey?

written 1923, one of the works published under the title
"Two Songs from Mexico" in *The Measure*, January 1924

II
Remembering Cuernavaca

And shall I hear again
Only in dreams the sound
Of water hurrying underground
To escape the greedy sun
And the Thirsting sky?
Or shall I
Discover fountains in this weaving sand
And cup a running river in my hand?

written 1923, unpublished

III
Fiesta de Santiago

He moves in the subtle trance
Of a wild delicate dance.
Masked in a smile of death
He lifts his hand
In a gesture scrawled upon tombs.
The odour of silence
Is in his breath.
He turns his head
With the fatal repose
Of the indifferent dead.

written 1923, published as one of "Two Songs from Mexico"
in *The Measure,* January 1924

[Lights on the river]

Lights on the river
Are thin daggers.
The walls of houses
Have cutting edges at corners
Where the jagged teeth of iron railings
Keep guard over nothing.
Under my feet the stones,
And on my heart
The dark rain falling.
O, rain, be merciful.
Wash away the sharp edges of the world.
Crumble under my feet the stones of my desolations.

written ca. 1924, unpublished

Now No Spring

For early tears and child's grief
Spring would send the shapely leaf;
For young grief and early sorrow
Summer brought a ripened furrow.

Now no Spring can set me free
From the thing that troubles me
And no summer soothe again
With its sleepy airs and rain
The winter-wakened scars of pain.

written ca. 1924, revised 15 February 1943, unpublished

Little Requiem

She should have had the state
Of a king's daughter,
Or a hut of willow branch
Near running water.

Or a scaled silver armour
For a breast cover,
Or a sweet lie in her mouth
For a lying lover.

Since she had none of these,
But a song instead,
She has well hidden herself
With the beaten dead.

Since for lack of these things
She knew herself lost,
She has well chosen silence
With her hands crossed.

published as "Requiescat—" in *The Measure,*
April 1924, retitled in *Collected Essays*

To a Portrait of the Poet

by Sor Juana Inés de la Cruz
translated from Spanish by Katherine Anne Porter

This which you see is merely a painted shadow
Wrought by the boastful pride of art,
With falsely reasoned arguments of colours,
A wary, sweet deception of the senses.

This picture, where flattery has endeavored
To mitigate the terrors of the years,
To defeat the rigorous assaults of Time,
And triumph over oblivion and decay—

Is only a subtle careful artifice,
A fragile flower of the wind,
A useless shield against my destiny.

It is an anxious diligence to preserve
A perishable thing: and clearly seen
It is a corpse, a whirl of dust, a shadow,—
      nothing.

published in *Survey Graphic,* May 1924

Procura desmentir los elogios que a un retrato de la poetisa inscribió la verdad, que llama pasión

by Sor Juana Inés de la Cruz

Este, que ves, engaño colorido,
que del arte ostentando los primores,
con falsos silogismos de colores
es cauteloso engaño del sentido;

este, en quien la lisonja ha pretendido
excusar de los años los horrores,
y venciendo del tiempo los rigores
triunfar de la vejez y del olvido,
        es un vano artificio del cuidado,
es una flor al viento delicada,
es un resguardo inútil para el hado:
        es una necia diligencia errada,
es un afán caduco y, bien mirado,
es cadáver, es polvo, es sombra, es nada.

reprinted in Trueblood's *A Sor Juana Anthology*
and in Porter's *Uncollected Early Prose*

November in Windham

These winds of Martinmas have stripped the trees
To cover the seeds of summer, and the limbs
Are rough as roots, and roots are cold as stone:
I catch my breath and shiver to the bone,
Blood-kinfolk to the crickets and the bees.

The deer have cut their trails in bedded leaves
Worm-bitter apples rot beside the wall,
The scanty crop is stored in loft and bin:
All day I feel the winter hurrying in,
All night the hunting owls cry at my eaves.

This is a country aching at the core,
Dead-tired of the year's labors, weary beyond sleep:
Seeded once more in stones again the yield
Of a forgotten scarecrow in a field
Set there to frighten birds that come no more[.]

written 1924–1926, published in *Harper's,*
November 1955

Winter Burial

Now crunches down the frozen stalk
On sterile snow:
Chill core of winter fruit in the mouth
Is bitter as a blow.

Pluck out this seed and bury it
Under a rock:
Against the winter measure of thin days
Tapped out upon a clock.

published in the *New York Herald Tribune,*
November 1926

First Episode

To M. J. [Matthew Josephson]

The roads seemed all alike and I could not
choose. There came a being who took my
hand and said: "I believe we are going in the
same direction. But for a time I feared we
might miss each other."

A secret
laid upon the mouth
in that day became an image.
O, image of imaginary loves
Imperfectly remembered pretexts for wisdom.

By what violence am I delivered
from how many bondages of speech
of tears of foreseeing.

This is a perilous place.
I have seen this place in dreams
and in the eyes of the dying.
I do not comprehend these presences—
Look again, look again you shall see
Strange signs in the fire and in the stars
In herbs and simples, in portentous stones.
There is no cure in them: console yourself with vows
Or pronounce maledictions.

A curse on all wounding things:
On terror on loneliness on mutilations—
All things edged, all thorns
All sharpened steel, all dividing waters
All clawed and fanged creatures
And all traps inviting their blind feet

He said: In the end a word shall be spoken
          And we shall listen:
          We shall give separate answers
          And one will not hear the other
          The end is not merciful.
          Let us hurry away silently
          Let us breathe innerly without stir
          Lest a leaf shake and arouse the sleeper.

written ca. 1928–1929, unpublished

Morning Song

He speaks:
  Come, my laid lady, whom I wooed with words,
   And called my Star—
Since you proved that you loved me, I
   Know what you are.

For, knowing what I am, I have a rod
   To measure by
If you mistake what I gave you for love, you are
   More beast than I.

And having eased in you my ambiguous lusts
   I now can prove
That you're a dupe who let me wallow you
   And call it love.

If I have feet of clay, yet you are now
   The dirt they trod—
And in that moment when I brought you down,
   I was a god!

written ca. 1929, unpublished

Night Blooming Cereus

Upborne by savage dark thorns the paper-lace dramatic flower
Spins in the winds, a dancing somnambulist;
With only a sleep walking witness, no audience for this hour.
The watchful birds are asleep, and the great fist

Of blackness closes leaving within itself no hollow.
There is no breath in this blackness; walk in your sleep and
    follow
Down to the sea's brim the promise of day, of the morning
Which rises again from the deep; shall not fail, will give warning.

Evening thou bringest all that bright morning scattered,
The bleating flock, the scrambling goats that stray,
And the young child that on the hillrocks scampered,
Comes weary to his mother from his play.

written 1929, unpublished

West Indian Island

Upborne by savage dark thorns the paper lace dramatic flower
Blooming in darkness, hangs from the rock like a dancer
Smiling blindly at her own image, mirrored in darkness.
All the long day the bees cling to the oleanders,
Pomegranates nod their heads, drowse, slowly turn scarlet.
Tree frogs cry from the gloom of arbors,
The great hand descends, doubling itself to a hollow.

Morning comes again after what a long night, and the ships
Hardly ripple the lost blue beside the coral;
At noon a flat meadow rises in the clouds, lies serenely
Speckled with sheep and low trees, and a narrow river
Hangs over the sea and smiles at its own image:
The mirrored face of illusion.
    O never shall I smile blindly at my own image,
Mirrored in darkness, in water, in clouds, in the faces of flowers,
It was never myself I loved, never this solitude,
Never this landscape without figures, this darkness, this water,
This shape that sits in famished pride staring at water,
At ships, at pomegranates, at moons, at oleanders,
Listening to tree frogs and the flying hooves of horses,
The sleepy whimper of birds, the rattle of rain on the palm
    leaves,
Fearing shadows and strange sounds and the white browed cliff
    and the darkness
Which never ends, yet ends in the promise of another darkness
    beginning
Blacker than the other: it was never my asking,
This pride and this fear and this solitude embodied and fixed,
Staring at water, at ships, at moons, at oleanders. . . . .

    O Island, loosen your roots, take to the sea,
    Leap the waves like a ship, nose bravely through storms,

Leave the hurricane whirling upon itself, let me return thus
To a familiar country.
      Quiet, severe, clothed in pain, full of memories,
Yet tranquil, never having sat staring,
At unshared loveliness, at averted warmth, at cruel softness,
    never
Having listened to music of strange instruments, never having
Plucked from strange air the breath of being,
This land
Will receive me as a friend, as a member
Of the family, will not mock at my journeys, nor recall them to
    me, nor deny them,
But will say easily, "So, daughter, you are late,
But come in, and welcome!"

The Hurricane.

    The storm seizes the loosened shutters, slips fingers
    sharper than glass under the panes,
Snatches away refuge, bends trees head to heels, rips the claws
    of birds
From their branches.
          So comes God straddling the whirlwind
Boasting, This is my power, but see!
I do not altogether abuse it. I am merciful
To the weak, to the sick, the hungry, the despised, the poor in
    spirit.
          Lord, what have I to do with such mercy?
Take the roof, the floor, the wall, the ground from under my
    feet,
Snatch away your firmament, drain your seas,
They are yours, you made them,
Take them again, I have no claim on them.
But what is mine, I keep.

Recession.

So then this contest with a mythical God goes on,
This endless debate with shadow, this
Colloquy between invented powers and imagined rebellions.
Now at high noon, there is calm again, with the grass flattened,
Under the receded flood, the broken armed trees still standing,
Sea-Salt rubbed in their wounds, but silent, but mystified,
To their hearts, but wondering,
And I say, "Brother, I wonder with you."
Who shall explain, who shall offer apology
To the great frogs spread belly white upon the muddy
Green banks, to the birds flattened to earth, wings
Spread still in the miraculous shapes of flying?

written 1929, unpublished

Music of the Official Jarabe and Versos

Collected in the State of Hidalgo
translated from the Spanish by Katherine Anne Porter

How lovely to dance the Jarabe
With rebozo and wide sombrero,
Dressed as China Poblano and Charro
And a sarape the color of morelia.

What a lovely dance is the Jarabe!
What a handsome lad is the Charro;
What a pretty girl is the China;
How beautiful it is to dance!

If you really love,
If you really love me,
First you have to teach me
How to make love
And when I get some money
We shall go and get married.

Come in and drink atole,
All of you passers-by.
If the atole is fresh and sweet
The atole maker is getting sour.

All the world approves
Of this milk of atole,
And good fat tamales,
And so it is no sin.

Indita, Indita, Indita,
The police have grabbed us!
You must go to the Rescue House,
And I to the jail must go.

Indita, Indita, Indita.
I come to ask a favor
Go look for another lover
Because I am going to marry.

The godmother is a rose,
The Godfather is a carnation,
The bride is a snivelly brat
And the groom is certainly one.

The dove and his mate
Went to confession together
And came back by the same road
Because they don't know how to pray.

Turn about and let us go!

published in *Mexican Folkways*, 1930

Música del Jarabe Oficial y Versos

Recogidos en el Estado de Hidalgo

Que bonito es bailar el jarabe
Con rebozo y sombrero jarano,
Con vestidos de China y de Charro
Y un sarape color moreliano.

Que bonito es el Jarabe;
Qué bonito es ese Charro,
Qué bonita es esa China,
Qué bonito es bailar todos.

Si usted me quiere de formalidad,
Si usted me quiere de formalidad,
Me ha de enseñar

El modo de enamorar,
Y cuando tengo dinero
Podremos irnos juntos a casar.

Pasen a tomar atole,
Todos los que van pasando,
Que si el atole está bueno,
La atolera se está agriando.

De este atolito de leche,
Y tamales de manteca,
Todo el mundo se aprovecha
Y por eso no se peca.

Indita, indita, indita,
La ronda nos agarró,
Tu irás a la recogida
Que yo a la cárcel me voy.

Indita, indita, indita,
Te vengo a solicitar,
Que busques amores nuevos,
Porque me voy a casar.

La madrina es una rosa,
El padrino es un clavel,
La novia es una mocosa
El novio por cierto es.

La paloma y el palomo
Se fueron a confesar,
Del camino se volvieron
Porque no sabían rezar

Da la vuelta y vámonos.

Bouquet for October

This is not our season, the spring-born
Put on winter like a hair shirt, remember death and wait
For the turn of the year.

It is not timely to say once for all
What love is. (Once for all words are engraved
On monuments celebrating potbellied kings, high-bosomed
　　ladies,
Philosophers, clowns, slender pages with crossed ankles,
Knights clasping with smooth knuckles
Blunted answerable arguments of heroics;
Above all, on the tombs of Statesmen.)

Streets of burnished iron, tender grass
Neatly shaven to the grey lips of water,
Hotels, cinemas, the loud cold shudders of ships,
The spouting of whales, the pocked jaws of friars, the orchestra
　　of machinery,
All all such memories are rayed metal, each shears off in turn
One minute from another, I must lose them all
Unless we make a sheaf of them together.

Landscapes such as the Flemish painted are justly
Asleep among windmills, thick with the smell
Of warm milk-soaked hides, ruminant breathings, clean orderly
　　hoofs,
Minute proprieties of doorways curtained with wood smoke,
Shaded away from clotted sky, winter thick water,
Numbed with certainties, snoring in a snowdrift.

If the frost stiffens our hair, we have still the taste
Of sun in our teeth.

The sea has hauled us by the shoulders over and under.
We have stretched our muscles and yawned in the smell of
cedar.

Catalogues of defeat, advantages stratagems, successes, anticipa-
tions,
Dried glories under glass, honors, a point of view petrified on its
feet,
I would leave in my will for whom such things are substance.
We will walk in the Tiergarten: invisible
To the little eyes buttoned up against the frail sunlight:
Observe the dubious riches of decay, pity
The bereaved branches, the exhausted leaves dropping
Like tears which nobody notices.

This is not our season, the spring-born
Wear winter like a thorn wreath, sniff the wind
For the earliest rumor of sap, the singing
Thaw of rivers, feel under their ribs
The snap of locks when the earth turns
The key to her wine vaults and the wines flow upwards.

Here on a marble bench we are at peace to mingle the ashes
Of our cigarettes, and to exchange our tokens:
A peach stone for a pigeon feather, a grasshopper wing for a sea
shell.

written 1931, published in *Pagany*, Winter 1932

94

Katherine Anne Porter's French Song-Book

Note

My choice of these particular songs for a small collection is neither arbitrary nor casual. First, I wished to make a singing version in English of French songs ranging over a period of about six hundred years; second, each song should be fairly representative of its time, and there should be only one song of a kind, such as a Carol, a Ballad, a Complaint, a Legend, a Brunette. Among these kinds I chose first for musical beauty, next for poetical and historical interest. In the end I chose always the special song that most appealed to me. This is the peculiar happy privilege of the collector, without which no one would ever be tempted to such an enterprise. The book is therefore a medley of the familiar, the famous, the popular, the obscure, the almost lost: but there is no song here that has not at one time or another been greatly known and loved; not one that has lost its meaning in spite of the differences of their luck in the mysterious chances of human favor.

There was no searching of the archives for recondite treasure. I consulted only a half-dozen song-books such as are published in France, a rich and wonderful jumble of songs meant to be sung and enjoyed, usually somewhat disfigured by trite accompaniments meant for the family piano. For much help and advice in the matter of Old French, and in the translation of Gilles Durant's poem, and for finding me the original version of Adam Billaut's song, I offer my gratitude to Mr. Willard Trask.

K. A. P.
Paris, May 15, 1933

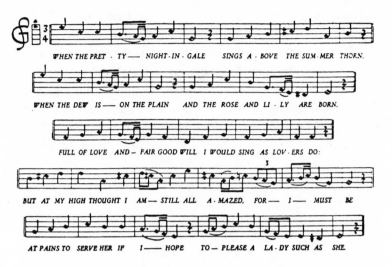

WHEN THE PRET · TY — NIGHT·IN·GALE   SINGS A · BOVE THE SUM·MER THORN.

WHEN THE DEW IS— ON THE PLAIN   AND THE ROSE AND LI · LY   ARE BORN.

FULL OF LOVE AND— FAIR GOOD WILL   I WOULD SING AS LOV·ERS DO:

BUT AT MY HIGH THOUGHT I   AM— STILL ALL   A·MAZED,   FOR—   I—   MUST   BE

AT PAINS TO SERVE HER IF   I—— HOPE   TO— PLEASE A   LA·DY SUCH AS SHE.

Morning Song for the Dame de Fayel

by the Chatelain de Coucy (1157–1192)

The most famous of the early troubadours; poet, singer, com-
poser, soldier, nobleman: a lucky being of many gifts and one
love. His spectacular and hopeless devotion to the Dame de
Fayel became legendary even in his lifetime, and flowered at
his death into one of the most celebrated of lovers' myths.

With his genius for the superlative, he did not take part in
any ordinary Crusade, but went to the Holy Land with Rich-
ard the Lion-hearted, and was there wounded fatally by a poi-
soned arrow in the last great battle with the Saracens, only a
short time before Richard made final truce with Saladin.

In the hour of his death he commanded that his heart should
be sent in a silver box as his last offering to the Dame de Fayel.
But the box fell into the hands of the Seigneur de Fayel, who
with the ingenuity of natural malice aggravated by long jeal-
ousy, caused the heart to be prepared and served to the lady at
table. She was then told what food she had eaten, and vowed
to touch no other food afterward, and so starved herself to

death: or leaped, say other chroniclers, to an instant death from her window.

This song must be among the earliest of the Chatelain's long service to his love, for many survive, and they move steadily from this dew on the green plain, this morning freshness, to despair and a vow of silence. In one of his last songs he asks pardon for his folly, saying his heart had deceived him knowingly, that his desire had been a joyous one, and since he is no longer joyous he can no longer sing.

When the pretty nightingale
Sings above the summer thorn,
When the dew is on the plain
And the rose and lily are born,

Full of love and fair good will
I would sing as lovers do:
But at my high thought I am still
All amazed, for I must be
At pains to serve her if I hope
To please a lady such as she.

Chanson du Chatelain de Coucy

Quand li roussignol joli
Chante sur la flor d'esté,
Que nait la rose et le li,
Et la rousée au vert pré,
Plein de bonne volonté,
Chanterai com fins amis;
Mais autant suis ébahi
Que j'ai si très haut pensé
Qu'a peine iert accompli
Li servirs dont j'attends gré.

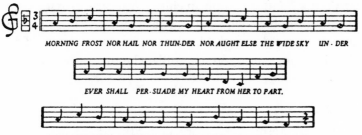

MORNING FROST NOR HAIL NOR THUN·DER NOR AUGHT ELSE THE WIDE SKY UN·DER

EVER SHALL PER·SUADE MY HEART FROM HER TO PART.

WHOM FULL LONG MY LOVE HATH SOUGHT WITH STEAD·FAST THOUGHT.

Lament

by Thibaut, Count of Champagne,
King of Navarre (1201–1254)

He was born nine years after the death of the Chatelain de Coucy, but in spite of the long generation separating them, each in turn was the flower of the High Middle Ages, and there is a deep similarity in their histories and temperaments.

Thibaut of Champagne was a great and arrogant nobleman, the most distinguished swordsman, poet and musician of his day. He made this melancholy song, and many others like it, for Queen Blanche, regent of France and mother of St. Louis. He allied himself with the Queen against the rebellious confederacy of great Vassals, and helped her secure the throne for her son. She sent her own army to help Thibaut defeat their common enemy, and he gave her the counties of Blois, Chartres, and Sancerre. In all, the fullness of his youth and manhood was devoted, with proper courtesy and most present helpfulness, to unrewarded love for his elect lady: "He loved her sweet look and beautiful face," says an annalist of the times, "and the sweetness of love took possession of his heart. But when he considered that she was of fair fame and good life, he silenced his thoughts of love in a profound sorrow. He made the most beautiful and melodious songs ever known."

In 1239, in a monstrous fit of piety, he caused one hundred and eighty-three heretics to be burned "on Mount Aime, near Vertus," and set off on an eighteen-month crusade with a company of nobles, who got only as far as Gaza in Palestine, where they were defeated. Thibaut returned to France and died in 1254, having survived Queen Blanche by nearly two years.

❧

Morning frost nor hail nor thunder
Nor aught else the wide sky under
Ever shall persuade my heart
　From her to part,
Whom full long my love hath sought
　With steadfast thought.

Fair thou art beyond all measure,
Thy contentment is my pleasure.
God, that all my love for thee
　Were thine for me!
When I pray, if she deny,
　Then must I die.

Pour Mal Tems, Ni Pour Gelée

Pour mal tems, ni pour gelée,
Ni pour froide matinée,
Ne partirai ma pensée
D'amour que j'ai;
Que trop l'ai aimée
De coeur verai!

Belle et blonde et colourée,
Moi plait quand nul vous agrée,
El die que me fut donnée
(Quand vous priai)
L'amour que vous ai vouée;
Je m'en morrai!

RO · BIN — LOVES ME. MY HEART'S HIS.

RO · BIN, WHEN HE COMES TO — ASK ME, SHALL HAVE "YES."

DEAREST — RO · BIN, NOTHING SPARING, EVERY SUN · DAY FOR MY PAIRING

BRINGS SOME PRETTY PIECE OF WEARING, NOTHING A —— MISS!

RO · BIN — LOVES ME. MY HEART'S HIS.

RO · BIN, WHEN HE COMES TO — ASK ME, SHALL HAVE "YES."

Marion's Song

by Adam de la Hale (1240–1287)

He was born the year that Thibaut, Count of Champagne, re-
turned from the Crusade, and lived through the reign of St.
Louis, but his mind was not on the Holy Sepulchre, or hope-
less love, or sainthood. He found in the elegant and festive
court of Charles of Anjou, the Saint's brother, at Naples, a
climate more sympathetic to his spirit, and he brought with
him many delightful novelties to charm the eyes and ears of his
audience.

Adam de la Hale was a true innovator. He wrote the first
French opera, "Le Jeu de Robins et Marion" and the first French
comedy, "Le Jeu de la Feuillée" and he filled them with the

101

old peasant airs, and popular songs of the towns, and rustic dances. He strung his borrowed melodies together on a simple plot, and the plot itself he owed to the early medieval Pastourelle, which had for its unchanging theme the love of a knight for a shepherdess or any simple country maid: They meet for the first time in a great wood or meadow, and the knight instantly offers his love, which the maid does, or does not, accept. It is, in fact, the other side of chivalry, the peasant's wistful view, the history of the knight's smaller loves with which he consoled himself for his unattainable lady.

This lovely song is from the opera, "Le Jeu de Robins et Marion" and the ancient plot has one important variation: Robin is not a knight but a country lad, and Marion is an honest maid far from coquetry or hesitation. She sings: "Robin has asked for me, and he shall have me!" Robin, too, has a comic song of courtship in which one question leads to another: he offers Marion a handsome paté, which they shall eat together, mouth to mouth. "Would you have more of me?" he inquires, and she answers frankly, "Yes, for the love of God." So he offers her a fat capon, which will not quite do either, and the dialogue goes on, its double meaning growing broader and broader.

This kind of rustic gayety was something new at court. Adam de la Hale prospered, wrote rondels, part-songs, motets, experimented with new harmonies, and his melodies, it was said, had more *music* in them than any other songs in the world. He was altogether unlike any other musician before him, and French music was in his debt for three hundred years.

I was happy to learn that he did not enter a monastery at the end of his life, as had been said.

ຂ໌ຂ

Robin loves me,
My heart's his.
Robin, when he comes to ask me,
Shall have "Yes."

Dearest Robin, nothing sparing,
Every Sunday for my fairing
Brings some pretty piece of wearing.

Nothing amiss!

Robin loves me,
My heart's his.
Robin, when he comes to ask me,
Shall have "Yes."

Robins M'Aime

Robins m'aime, Robins m'a,
    Robins m'a demandée
        Si m'ara.

Robins m'acata cotèle
D'escarlate bone et bèle,
Souskranie et chainturèle
    A leur i va.
Robins m'aime, Robins m'a;
    Robins m'a demandée
        Si m'ara.

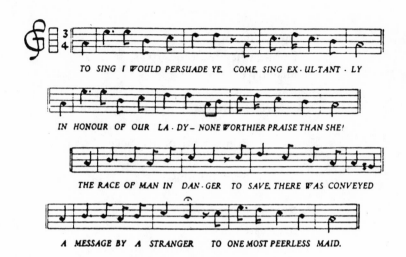

TO SING I WOULD PERSUADE YE. COME, SING EX·UL·TANT·LY

IN HONOUR OF OUR LA·DY— NONE WORTHIER PRAISE THAN SHE!

THE RACE OF MAN IN DAN·GER TO SAVE, THERE WAS CONVEYED

A MESSAGE BY A STRANGER TO ONE MOST PEERLESS MAID.

Sing, I Pray You

carol
anonymous (ca. 1500)

This poem in praise of Mary is very ancient, being older than the music which accompanies it, and it is found in many early collections, set to various melodies, most of them having originated as love songs, or dance tunes. This air is recorded from 1550, and is on the solemn order of the true Noël, or hymn sung on the entrances of Kings, and at other high feasts. . . . . .

❧

To sing I would persuade ye,
  Come, sing exultantly
In honor of Our Lady—
  None worthier praise than she!
The race of man in danger
  To save, there was conveyed
A message by a stranger
  To one most peerless maid.

And Mary she was naméd,
  As destined so to be,
Of royal stock and faméd,
  The fruit of Jesse's tree.
Now tell us, Lady Mary,
  What name he bore who gave
The glorious tidings to thee,
  Which all the world shall save.

Chantons Je Vous en Prie

Chantons je vous en prie,
Par exaltation,
En l'honneur de Marie
Pleine de grand renom.
Pour tout l'humain lignage
Jeter hors de péril,
Fut transmis un message
A la vierge de prix.

Marie fut nommée
Par destination,
De royale lignée
Par generation,
Or nous dites Marie
Qui fut le messager
Qui porta la nouvelle,
Pour le monde sauver.

'LAS! IN MY LOVELY SPRING, YEA, WHEN MY YOUTH SHOULD FLOWER,

FEEL I AN INWARD STING, TURNS ALL MY SWEET TO SOUR.

HEART, FORSAKING PLEASURE, COUNTETH SORROW TREA — SURE.

Mary Stuart's Plaint for Her Youth

by Mary Stuart, Queen of Scots (1542–1587)

Brantôme recorded that Mary Stuart "wrote this song, when, to her great regret, she had been about eighteen months in Scotland." Later specialists in minutiae have denied this, giving in turn to David Rizzio, her secretary, who was a first-rate musician; to du Caurroy, Chapel Master to Charles IX, Henry III, and Henry IV; and to unknown persons, the honor of writing Mary Stuart's songs. The French court was alive with poet-musicians, royal or professional, but Mary Stuart was distinguished among them for the songs she composed, as well as for her way of singing them to her own accompaniment on the lute or the virginal. Since those persons who lived nearest to her professed to believe she wrote this Plaint, and since it is so clearly the kind of song she might have written, one may as well think it is hers, until some zealous researcher can name the real composer.

106

'Las! in my lovely spring,
Yea, when my youth should flower,
Feel I an inward sting,
Turns all my sweet to sour.
Heart, forsaking pleasure,
Counteth sorrow treasure.

Whether I walk the fields
Or hide me in the forest,
Morning or evening yields
Unto my grieving no rest—
Heart is still alone:
Whom it seeketh, gone.

Las! En Mon Doux Printems

Las! en mon doux printems
Et fleur de ma jeunesse,
Toutes les peines sens
D'une extrême tristesse,
Et en rien n'ai plaisir,
Qu'en regret et désir.

Si en quelque séjour,
Soit en bois ou en prée,
Soit à l'aube du jour,
Ou soit à la vesprée,
Sans cesse mon coeur sent
Le regret d'un absent!

MY GA-BRIELLE, TO CHARM ME MORE STRONG THAN ALL THE STARS —

WHEN FAME AND GLO-RY ARM ME AND BID ME FOL-LOW MARS.

HOW BITTER IS THAT SENDING, I CAN — BUT SIGH —

AND ONE MUST HAVE AN ENDING: MY LOVE, OR I.

In Praise of Gabrielle d'Estrée

by King Henry IV of France (1553–1610),
music by du Caurroy

King Henry IV, unlike Thibaut, Count of Champagne, was ever so much better at fighting than at making verse. But he seems to have been unaware of it and placed this song, full of warrior's boasting and military figures of speech, at the feet of Gabrielle d'Estrée.

There are some sour spirits who presume even to doubt that the King wrote the words, but it is certain that du Caurroy wrote the music. That was his business at court, and he wrote love songs for three kinds in succession. . . . . .

My Gabrielle, to charm me
More strong than all the stars—
When fame and glory arm me
And bid me follow Mars,

How bitter is that sending,
   I can but sigh—
And one must have an ending:
   My love, or I!

Love—and if 'tis a wonder
'Tis you thereof may boast—
Has, like a great commander,
Enrolled me in his host.

   How bitter, etc.

I did, in war's hot fire
A single kingdom gain.
But 'tis the earth entire
O'er which your eyes should reign.

   How bitter, etc.

Fair star I lose—oh sadness,
Oh cruel memory,
My sorrow grows to madness.
I must return, or die.

   How bitter, etc.

Charmante Gabrielle

Charmante Gabrielle,
Percé de mille dards,
Quand la Gloire m'appelle
A la suite de Mars!
Cruelle départie,
   Malheureux jour!
Que ne suis-je sans vie,
   Ou sans amour!

L'Amour, sans nulle peine,
M'a, par vos doux regards,
Comme un grand capitaine,
Mis sous ses étendards.
Cruelle départie, etc.

Je n'ai pu, dans la guerre,
Qu'un royaume gagner,
Mais sur toute la terre,
Vos yeux doivent régner.
Cruelle départie, etc.

Bel astre que je quitte,
Ah, cruel souvenir!
Ma douleur s'en irrite . . .
Vous revoir ou mourir!
Cruelle départie, etc.

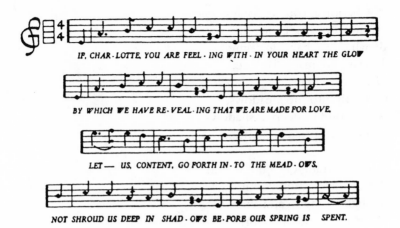

IF, CHAR-LOTTE, YOU ARE FEEL-ING WITH-IN YOUR HEART THE GLOW

BY WHICH WE HAVE RE-VEAL-ING THAT WE ARE MADE FOR LOVE.

LET — US, CONTENT, GO FORTH IN-TO THE MEAD-OWS,

NOT SHROUD US DEEP IN SHAD-OWS BE-FORE OUR SPRING IS SPENT.

To Charlotte

poem
by Gilles Durant (1550–1615). Musician unknown

Gilles Durant, one of the most gifted poets at the French Court, was almost an exact contemporary of King Henry IV, and his life as poet coincided fairly with the Elizabethans, to whom he was a less robust blood-brother. This sentimental and exceedingly refined poem is in the most fashionable feeling of his time and place: as far from the romantic pride in sacrificial devotion of the early royal troubadours as from the jolly mutual rustic comedy of Robin and Marion. He lacks, too, the childish heartlessness of the English lyrists, who urge their mistresses to be kind now, during their brief opportunity, for tomorrow they will find themselves neglected for fresher roses. This poet shares his fears with the beloved, it is for them both that death and darkness wait. The invitation is full of listless longing and vague tenderness, and the air, probably by du Caurroy, is delicate as a sigh.

❧

If, Charlotte, you are feeling
Within your heart the glow
By which we have revealing
That we are made for love,
  Let us, content,
Go forth into the meadows,
Not shroud us deep in shadows
Before our spring is spent.

While morning does but waken,
Before our fleeting youth
By night being overtaken
Is lost in shades uncouth,
  Let us take time
To fill our lives with solace
Nor fear at all, though jealous,
Some name our pleasures crime.

The sun, in splendor burning,
Has, every night, his wane,
Then, at the dawn's returning,
Shines glorious again.
  Our little light
When once it has its setting,
Forgotten and forgetting,
Lies closed in endless night.

Ma Belle Si Ton Ame . . .

Ma belle si ton âme
Se sent or allumer
De cette douce flamme
Qui nous force d'aimer,
  Allons contens,
Allons sur la verdure,

Allons tandis que dure
Notre jeune printems.

Avant que la journée
De notre âge qui fuit
Se trouve environnée
Des ombres de la nuit,
  Prenons loisir
De vivre notre vie,
Et sans craindre l'envie
Donnons-nous du plaisir!

Du soleil la lumière
Vers le soir se déteint,
Puis à l'aube première
Elle reprend son teint;
  Mais notre jour,
Quand une fois il tombe,
Demeure sous la tombe
Sans espoir de retour.

AN · Y HOUR, AN · Y WEATHER, NIGHT OR DAY OR RAIN OR SHINE,

STILL I KEEP THE BOTTLE BUZZING, STILL I KEEP THE BOTTLE BUZZING,

STILL MY ON · LY LOVE IS WINE.

Drinking Song

by Adam Billaut (d. 1662)

A carpenter of Nevers, who wrote such lively poetry he won the title of Master Adam from his admirers, and whose drinking songs are much more than mere drunken yells of delight at seeing another cask broached. A profound, one might almost say sober, appreciation of the beauties and benefits of good wine is in his song, mingled with scraps of classical allusion and a knowing glance at the charms of nature. The Master was no mere loose-kneed bibber, but a prideful artisan as well as poet, and he mingled the two vocations without effort, so that one enriched the other. He divided his volume of poems into sections with such heads as: The Saw, the Adze, the Chisel, the Hammer, the Plane, and so to the end, slighting no member of his carpenter's chest. . . . . He received much honor from his fellow verse-makers, who dedicated doggerel to him in many dead and living languages; he was called the "Virgil au rabot" and was praised by the great Corneille. Enough.

It was once believed, and is now denied, that Master Adam wrote the music for his song, and it was much commended as an ideal marriage of words and melody. I found it rather dull, as compared with another tune, of uncertain origin, which carried words altogether unworthy of it. So I have re-wedded Master Adam's words to this more reckless melody, and the result is quite another song. In doing this, I am merely observing faithfully an ancient tradition, and, I think, a very good and useful one.

&

Any hour, any weather,
Night or day or rain or shine,
Still I keep the bottle buzzing,   *(bis)*
Still my only love is wine.

Serving under General Bacchus,
Not a single care have I
But to hear my belly grumble   *(bis)*
Sometimes, when the cask runs dry.

Dawn no sooner gilds my vineyard,
On the hill-side where it basks,
Than I feel I must be drinking—   *(bis)*
Down I go to wake my casks.

Glass in hand I greet the morning,
Then this question I propose:
"Phoebus, tell me, can Golconda   *(bis)*
Show more rubies than my nose?"

If the Fates could be so kindly
As with drink to stop my breath,
Not for all that life can give me   *(bis)*
Would I change so good a death.

Down Hell's highway I should hasten,
Drink the Furies to a doze,
Then set up a cozy tavern   *(bis)*
Under Pluto's very nose.

When I'm seated at my table,
Food on plate and wine in stoup,
Let all threateners—be they princes—   *(bis)*
Save their breaths to cool their soup!

Nought has power to confound me.
When I tipple, do I hear
Jupiter in heaven thunder?—   *(bis)*
Well I know 'tis out of fear.

Could the pestilential ocean,
Filled with fish and salt and cold,
Claim but any kind of kinship   *(bis)*
With the juice my barrels hold,

I could find it in my nature,
Bravely rowing in a skiff,
Solemnly to leave the shore and   *(bis)*
Wreck myself against some cliff.

Neither gold nor bronze nor marble
For my monument I ask;
Rather let my simple coffin   *(bis)*
Be the roundness of a cask.

Underneath my ruddy portrait,
Set these verses of my own:
"Here lies one, the greater toper   *(bis)*
That the world has ever known."

Chanson Bachique

Que Phébus soit dedans l'onde
Ou dans son oblique tour,
Je bois toujours à la ronde;
Le vin est tout mon amour:
Soldat du fils de Sémèle,
Tout le tourment qui me poinct,
C'est quand mon ventre grommelle,
Faute de ne boire point.

Aussitost que le lumière,
A redoré nos coteaux,
Je commence ma carrière
Par visiter mes tonneaux.
Ravi de revoir l'aurore,
Le verre en main je lui dis:
"Vois-tu sur la rive more
Plus qu'à mon nez de rubis?"

Si quelque jour, étant ivre,
La Parque arrête mes pas,
Je ne veux point, pour revivre,
Quitter un si doux trépas.
Je m'en irai dans l'Averne
Faire enivrer Alecton,
Et planterai ma taverne
Dans la chambre de Pluton.

Le plus grand de la terre,
Quand je suis au repas,
S'il m'annonçoit la guerre,
Il n'y gagneroit pas;
Jamais je ne m'etonne;

Et je crois, quand je boi,
Que si Jupiter tonne,
C'est qu'il a peur de moi.

Si l'humide partie
Du sejour des poissons
Alloit en sympathie
Au jus de nos poinçons,
Sans doute mon courage
Ne pourroit s'empescher
D'aller faire naufrage
Contre quelque rocher!

De marbre ni de porphyre
Qu'on ne fasse mon tombeau;
Pour cercueil je ne désire
Que le contour d'un tonneau;
Je veux qu'on peigne ma trogne
Avec ces vers à l'entour:
"Ci-gît le plus grand ivrogne
Qui jamais ait vu le jour."

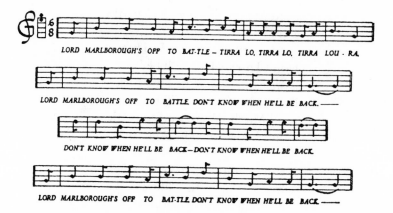

LORD MARLBOROUGH'S OFF TO BAT-TLE — TIRRA LO, TIRRA LO, TIRRA LOU - RA.

LORD MARLBOROUGH'S OFF TO BATTLE DON'T KNOW WHEN HE'LL BE BACK. —

DON'T KNOW WHEN HE'LL BE BACK — DON'T KNOW WHEN HE'LL BE BACK.

LORD MARLBOROUGH'S OFF TO BAT-TLE DON'T KNOW WHEN HE'LL BE BACK. —

Marlborough

satirical ballad
from the French-English War
of the Spanish Succession (1703–1713)

Whatever other results might be, every war between France and England has always produced, on the French side, a fresh crop of witty and scandalous songs about the English. Of them all, this anonymous satire (or the words, at least: there is no knowing how old the tune may be), an echo of the long unpleasantness between Queen Anne and King Louis XIV, has become international, and the English sing it too, even with the original words, or, with other verses, as a drinking song. Before the melody became world-famous, it was a dolorous little love ditty, a kind of spinning song.

Unfortunately for the French, the rumor of Marlborough's death was a rumor merely, but we have the song, which was surely the best thing that came out of that war.

Lord Marlborough's off to battle—
Tirra lo, tirra lo, tirra loura,
Lord Marlborough's off to battle,
Don't know when he'll be back.
Don't know when he'll be back;
Don't know when he'll be back.
Lord Marlborough's off to battle,
Don't know when he'll be back.

He's coming back for Easter,
Tirra lo, tirra lo, tirra loura,
He's coming back for Easter,
Or else for Trinity.   *(Repeat last line three times; then
repeat last two lines.)*

But Trinity is over,
Tirra lo, tirra lo, tirra loura,
But Trinity is over,
And Marlborough doesn't come.

My lady climbs the tower
'Till there's no more to climb.

She sees his page a-running
In black from top to toe.

"You pretty page, come tell me
What news you run to bring."

"Such news I bring, My Lady,
As those fair eyes shall weep.

"Lay by your scarlet dresses,
Your rich brocaded silks.

"My Lord of Marlborough's dead,
Is dead and buriéd.

"I saw him carried slowly,
Carried by captains four.

"And one tall man his helmet
And one his shield did bring,

"And one tall man his sabre
And one did nothing bring.

"His marble tomb we planted
All round with rosemary.

"In all the highest branches
Sad nightingales did sing.

"We saw his soul ascending
Up through the laurel-wreaths.

"We fell upon our bellies
And then got up again,

"To sing the glorious conquests
Lord Marlborough always made.

"The ceremony over
We all went off to bed—

"And some of us with ladies
And others all alone.

"Not that there's any shortage,
I know of quite a few,

"Some dark and others lighter,
And even a red or two."

Malbrough

Malbrough s'en va-t-en guerre,
Mironton, mironton, mirontaine,
Malbrough s'en va-t-en guerre,
Ne sait quand reviendra,
Ne sait quand reviendra,
Ne sait quand reviendra.

Il reviendra à Pâques,
Mironton, mironton, mirontaine,
Il reviendra à Pâques
Ou à la Trinité.   (ter)

La Trinité se passe,
Mironton, mironton, mirontaine,
La Trinité se passe,
Malbrough ne revient pas.   (ter)

Madame à sa tour monte,
Si haut qu'ell' peut monter.

Elle aperçoit son page,
Tout de noir habillé:

"Beau page, mon beau page,
Quell' nouvelle apportez?"

—Aux nouvell's que j'apporte
Vos beaux yeux vont pleurer.

Quittez vos habits roses
Et vos satins brochés.

Monsieur Malbrough est mort,
Est mort et enterré.

J'lai vu porter en terre
Par quatre z'officiers.

L'un portait sa cuirasse,
L'autre son bouclier.

L'un portait son grand sabre,
L'autre rien ne portait.

A l'entour de sa tombe
Romarins l'on planta.

Sur la plus haute branche
Le rossignol chanta.

On vit voler son âme
Au travers des lauriers.

Chacun mit ventre à terre,
Et puis se releva.

Pour chanter les victoires
Que Malbrough remporta.

La Cérémonie faite
Chacun s'en fut coucher.

Les uns avec leurs femmes,
Et les autres tout seuls.

Ce n'est pas qu'il en manque,
Car j'en connais beaucoup.

Des brunes et des blondes
Et des châtaign's aussi.—

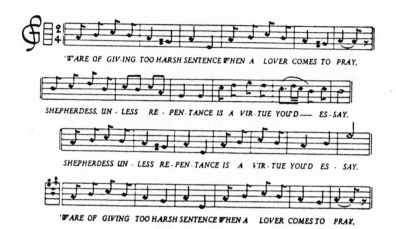

'WARE OF GIV-ING TOO HARSH SENTENCE WHEN A LOVER COMES TO PRAY.

SHEPHERDESS, UN - LESS RE - PEN-TANCE IS A VIR-TUE YOU'D — ES-SAY.

SHEPHERDESS UN - LESS RE-PEN-TANCE IS A VIR-TUE YOU'D ES - SAY.

'WARE OF GIVING TOO HARSH SENTENCE WHEN A LOVER COMES TO PRAY.

Shepherdess, Be Kind

brunette
anonymous (ca. 1700)

The Brunette is a special sort of playful small song of love at its lightest and most fickle, and was named for the little dark girls it usually celebrates. It has all the properties of a Bergerette: its affectedly rustic names, birds and forests and flowers and even a stray sheep or two: but it is not the same thing quite, and it lacks the knowing leer of the best Vaudeville.

Among the thousands of such songs, this one seems to wear best, as it is to be found in collections old and new, for children as well as for adults. . . . .

ε♣

'Ware of giving too harsh sentence
When a lover comes to pray,
Shepherdess, unless repentance
Is a virtue you'd essay.

Shepherdess, unless repentance
    Is a virtue you'd essay.
'Ware of giving too harsh sentence
    When a lover comes to pray.

'Ware of giving too harsh sentence
    When a lover comes to pray;
Pleasure doesn't dance attendance—
    Put it off, it flies away.

Pleasure doesn't dance attendance—
    Put it off, it flies away.
'Ware of giving too harsh sentence
    When a lover comes to pray.

Gardez-Vous D'Etre Sévère

Gardez-vous d'être sévère
Quand on vous parle d'amour,
Votre coeur, jeune bergère,
S'en repentirait un jour.

Gardez-vous d'être sévère
Quand on vous parle d'amour
Votre coeur, jeune bergère,
S'enrepentirait un jour.

Gardez-vous d'être sévère
Quand on vous parle d'amour,
Votre coeur, jeune bergère,
S'en repentirait un jour.

Un plaisir que l'on diffère
Se perd souvent sans retour:

Gardez-vous d'être sévère,
Quand on vous parle d'amour.

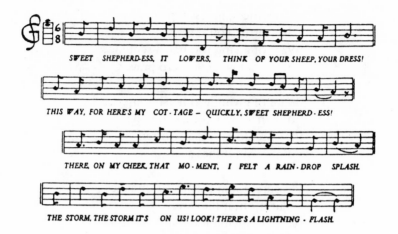

SWEET SHEPHERD-ESS, IT LOWERS, THINK OF YOUR SHEEP, YOUR DRESS!

THIS WAY, FOR HERE'S MY COT-TAGE - QUICKLY, SWEET SHEPHERD-ESS!

THERE, ON MY CHEEK, THAT MO-MENT, I FELT A RAIN-DROP SPLASH.

THE STORM, THE STORM IT'S ON US! LOOK! THERE'S A LIGHTNING-FLASH.

The Shower

bergerette
by Fabre d'Eglantine (1750–1794)

He was born in Carcassonne and his family name was Fabre. He added the second name to commemorate his first achievement, having received the golden eglantine in the Academy of Floral Games in Toulouse. Afterward he travelled about the provinces as an actor, writing poetry and plays meanwhile, and so won his way to Paris. He fell in with the young intellectuals and politicians who were fomenting the Revolution, wrote revolutionary satire into his plays, joined the Jacobin Club and was made president and secretary of the Club of the Cordeliers. Danton employed him as private secretary, and, probably, through this ferocious influence, Fabre became one of the most bloodthirsty of the terrorists: voted for the King's death, and thereafter for the death of anyone so unlucky as to be brought to trial, or even suspected of royalist sympathies. He invented most of the names for the months and days for the new Republican calendar, and continued to write somewhat. . . . .

On the eve of the fall of Danton, a charge of public malfeasance was trumped up against him by the Committee of Public Safety, which now hounded Dantonists as the Dantonists had hounded others, and Fabre was condemned to death. His actor's training and love for drama stood him in good stead at his trial: he carried himself with great self-possession, and sang his song, "Il pleut, il pleut, Bergère," well known then, but no better known than it is now. On the way to the scaffold, he scattered his manuscript poems to the People: that draggle-tailed mob who cared little whose death it was so they might see it, and nothing at all for his poetry. Judged by his last act, it is plain that he had always thought of himself primarily as a man of letters. . . . .

There are many verses more, telling, in the high-minded way made fashionable by Rousseau and the Revolution, of the blameless romance which followed this chance encounter between virtuous shepherd and innocent shepherdess in the storm. They are sweetly silly, and translation does not help them.

&

Sweet shepherdess, it lowers,
 Think of your sheep, your dress!
This way, for here's my cottage—
 Quickly, sweet shepherdess!

There, on my cheek, that moment,
 I felt a rain-drop splash.
The storm, the storm—it's on us!
 Look! There's a lightning-flash.

Il Pleut, Il Pleut, Bergère

Il Pleut, il pleut, bergère,
 Presse tes blancs moutons;
Allons sous ma chaumière,
 Bergère, vite allons!

J'entends sur le feuillage
 L'eau qui tombe à grand bruit;
Voici, voici l'orage,
 Voilà l'éclair qui luit.

127

"STRIKE UP, MY DRUMS," SO SPAKE THE KING, "STRIKE UP, MY DRUMS," SO SPAKE THE KING.

"SUMMON MY LADIES HI ———— THER."

SOUNDED THE DRUM, STRAIGHT COMETH ONE. WINNETH HIM AL · TO · GE ———— THER.

RA TA BOUM, RA TA BOUM, RA TA TA TA TA TA TA. RA TA BOUM, RA TA BOUM, RA TA TA TA TA TA TA.

The King Beats the Drum

legend

We have the evidence of fairy tales and of Russian Tsars until Peter the Great that once upon a time, when a king designed to marry, or to take a new mistress, he called for all the marriageable girls of his kingdom to be brought before him for his choice.

King Henry VIII, seeking to replace Queen Jane Seymour, then lately dead, suggested that a fine bevy of eligible young French ladies be brought to Calais for his personal inspection. It was not done, and one French envoy concerned in the negotiations commented to another: "To bring him thither as he asks, young ladies to choose and make them promenade on show! They are not hackneys to sell, and there would be no propriety in it!"

This legend is quite a complicated history of human passions and its myth is history by means of symbol. The verses have admirable precision and economy, in spite of their long life of floating from mouth to mouth. The vague anachronisms of detail do not in the least destroy the air of immense antiquity around this song.

"Strike up my drums," so spake the King,
"Summon my ladies hither."
Sounded the drum, straight cometh one,
Winneth him altogether.

Ra ta boum, ra ta boum, ra ta ta ta ta ta
Ra ta boum, ra ta boum, ra ta ta ta ta ta.

"Marquis, come forth! Knowest thou her?
Tell me her name, I pray thee."
Answer he made, "Sire, 'tis no maid,
But my own wedded lady."
      Ra ta boum, etc.

"Happier art thou, Marquis, than I,
Having so fair a lady;
Couldst thou agree, mine she should be,
I would maintain her bravely."

"Were not thy head saved by a crown,
Nothing, my liege, should save it.
But to the crown all must bow down,
Be it as thou wouldst have it."

"Come, be not grieved, Marquis, I say,
Lord Marshal now I make thee.
Nay, not a word. 'Tis thy reward.
Off, to thy post betake thee."

"Farewell my love, farewell my sweet,
Farewell my only treasure,
Farewell my heart, now we must part:
Such is thy sovereign's pleasure."

Quickly the Queen made a bouquet,
All of the lily flower.
Sweet was its scent. The lady bent,
Smelled, and lay dead that hour.

Le Roi a Fait Battre Tambour

Le roi a fait battre tambour . . .
Le roi a fait battre tambour
Pour voir toutes ses dames;
La première qu'il a vue
Lui a ravie son âme.

Ra-ta-plan, ra-ta-plan,
Ra-ta-plan, plan, plan, plan,
Ra-ta-plan, ra-ta-plan,
Rataplan, plan, plan, plan!

"Marquis, dis-moi, la connais-tu?
Marquis, dis-moi, la connais-tu?
Qui est cett' joli' dame?"
Le marquis lui a répondu:
"Sire roi, c'est ma femme."

"Marquis tu es plus heureux qu'moi   (bis)
D'avoir femme si belle,
Si tu voulais me l'accorder
Je me chargerais d'elle."

"Sire, si vous n'étiez le roi,   (bis)
J'en tirerais vengeance,
Mais puisque vous êtes le roi,
A votre obéissance."

"Marquis ne te fâche donc pas,   (bis)
T'auras ta récompense,

Dans mes armées tu seras
Beau maréchal de France."

"Adieu ma mie, adieu mon coeur,   (bis)
Adieu mon espérance!
Puisqu'il te faut servir le roi
Séparons-nous d'ensemble."

La reine a fait faire un bouquet   (bis)
De belles fleurs de lyse
Et la senteur de ce bouquet
Fit mourir la marquise.

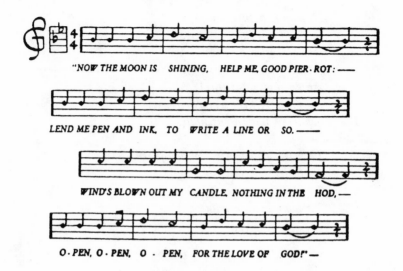

"NOW THE MOON IS SHINING, HELP ME, GOOD PIER-ROT: ——

LEND ME PEN AND INK, TO WRITE A LINE OR SO. ——

WIND'S BLOWN OUT MY CANDLE, NOTHING IN THE HOD, ——

O-PEN, O-PEN, O-PEN, FOR THE LOVE OF GOD!" ——

Full Moon

author and date unknown

This and the "Bridge of Avignon" are the two French songs which foreigners know, if they know two French songs. If they know only one, it will be one of these two. . . . .

❧

"Now the moon is shining,
        Help me, good Pierrot:
Lend me pen and ink, to
        Write a line or so.
Wind's blown out my candle,
        Nothing in the hod,
Open, open, open,
        For the love of God!"

"But the moon is shining,"
    Answered good Pierrot,
"Pen's lost. And I went to
    Bed three hours ago.
Ask the next-door neighbour,
    She's about, I think.
Seems to me I hear her
    Tapping at her flint."

While the moon is shining,
    Strephon, handsome swain,
Comes to Chloe's door, and
    Knocks and knocks again.
"Who comes here so late, sir?"
    Chloe asks above.
"Open, Chloe, open,
    For the God of love!"

Au Clair de la Lune

"Au clair de la lune,
Mon ami Pierrot,
Prête-moi ta plume
Pour écrire un mot.
Ma chandelle est morte,
Je n'ai plus de feu,
Ouvre-moi ta porte,
Pour l'amour de Dieu."

Au clair de la lune,
Peirrot répondit:
"Je n'ai pas de plume,
Je suis dans mon lit.
Va chez la voisine,

Je crois qu'elle y est,
Car dans la cuisine
On bat le briquet."

Au clair de la lune,
L'aimable Lubin
Frappe chez la brune,
Ell' repond soudain:
"Qui frapp' de la sorte?"
Il dit à son tour:
"Ouvre votre porte
Pour le dieu d'amour."

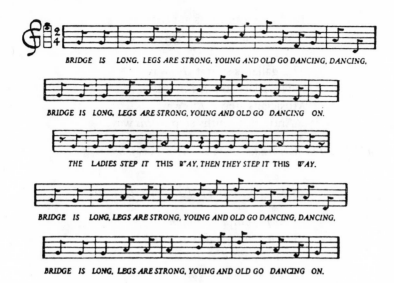

BRIDGE IS LONG, LEGS ARE STRONG, YOUNG AND OLD GO DANCING, DANCING,

BRIDGE IS LONG, LEGS ARE STRONG, YOUNG AND OLD GO DANCING ON.

THE LADIES STEP IT THIS WAY, THEN THEY STEP IT THIS WAY.

BRIDGE IS LONG, LEGS ARE STRONG, YOUNG AND OLD GO DANCING, DANCING,

BRIDGE IS LONG, LEGS ARE STRONG, YOUNG AND OLD GO DANCING ON.

Bridge of Avignon

ronde
author and date unknown

This is rather like including "The Farmer in the Dell" in a book
of English songs translated into French, but in such a book
"The Farmer in the Dell" should be included.

> Bridge is long, legs are strong,
>   Young and old go dancing, dancing,
> Bridge is long, legs are strong,
>   Young and old go dancing on.

The ladies step it *this* way, Then they step it *this* way.

> Bridge is long, legs are strong,
>   Young and old go dancing, dancing,

Bridge is long, legs are strong,
   Young and old go dancing on.

The gallants step it *this* way. . . . .
   The friars step it *this* way. . . . .
Musicians step it *this* way. . . . .
   And blacksmiths step it *this* way.

(Children put in other trades, imitating them as they sing.)

Sur Le Pont D'Avignon

Sur le pont d'Avignon
Tout le monde y danse, danse,
Sur le pont d'Avignon
Tout le monde y danse en rond.

Les beaux messieurs font comm' ça . . .

Sur le pont d'Avignon,
Tout le monde y danse, danse;
Sur le pont d'Avignon
Tout le monde y danse en rond.

Les capucins font comm' ça . . .

Sur le pont d'Avignon,
Tout le monde y danse, danse;
Sur le pont d'Avignon,
Tout le monde y danse en rond.

(Les enfants ajoutent tous les métiers qu'ils veulent et les imitent en chantant).

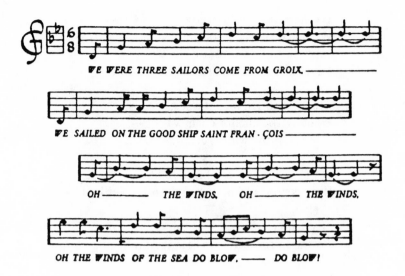

WE WERE THREE SAILORS COME FROM GROIX.

WE SAILED ON THE GOOD SHIP SAINT FRAN · ÇOIS

OH ——— THE WINDS, OH ——— THE WINDS,

OH THE WINDS OF THE SEA DO BLOW. —— DO BLOW!

The Three Sailors

anonymous
legend

An old Brittany sea song not so popular as it deserves to be. It exposes, with such a good tune and such dashing words, the tough spirit of the Breton sea-going men and the maternal commonsense, the frankness and firmness of their great patroness, Saint Anne. Being created to the pattern of their needs, she resembles rather a household goddess of pre-Christian times, versatile enough to rise, on occasion, from the sea. I have seen a beautiful porcelain figure of her holding her great cloak: curved like a sail before the wind, blue as fine weather, sprinkled with stars like a clear night, lined and bordered with the foam of a sea wave: spread protectingly over a group of small kneeling Bretons in their work-day dress, and at her feet the simple legend: "Saint Anne, Grandmother of the Bretons, watch over us."

We were three sailors come from Groix,—
We sailed on the good ship Saint François—
        Oh the winds, oh the winds,
Oh the winds of the sea do blow, do blow!

The second fell into the sea,
Hauling the anchor chair was he—
        Oh the winds, etc.

We found no more of him in life
But his pipe and his cap and his pocket knife—

His mama runs as fast as she can
To say a prayer to good Saint Anne—

Oh Saint Anne, give me back my son!
Said Saint Anne, such things can't be done—

Said Saint Anne, dry your weeping eyes,
You'll see him again in Paradise—

Les Trois Marins De Groix

Nous étions trois marins de Groix
Embarqués sur le Saint-François.
        Il vente, il vente:
C'est le vent de la mer qui nous tourmente!

En dérapant l'ancre de fer.
Mon matelot tombe à la mer
        Il vente, il vente, etc.

On n'a trouvé que son chapeau,
Son garde-pipe et son couteau.
        Il vente, il vente, etc.

Sa mère qui s'en va prier
La bonne sainte Anne d'Auray: . . .
Il vente, il vente, etc.

"Sainte Anne rendez-moi mon fils,"
La bonne sainte lui a dit: . . .
Il vente, il vente, etc.

La bonne sainte lui a dit:
"Tu le r'verras en paradis!"
Il vente, il vente:
C'est le vent de la mer qui nous tourmente.

MY MOTHER CHOSE MY HUSBAND; A LAWYER'S SON WAS HE.——

WHEN, ON THE WEDDING NIGHT HE CAME TO BED WITH ME,

AH, AH, AH! THAT'S NO WAY TO – AH, AH, AH! THAT CAN'T BE!

My Mother Chose My Husband

Old French songs are divided nicely into definite categories, such as Complaints, Rondes, Ballads, Minuets, Bergerettes, Vaudevilles: this song belongs to the highly specialised Complaints of the Ill-Married. The theme was familiar from the twelfth century at least, and was the favorite topic of street and bridge singers. "My Mother Chose my Husband" is fairly modern, but it comes of a long and voluble ancestry. Sometimes it is the husband who complains, and always of two things; his mother-in-law is a fiend, and his wife has made him a cuckold: sometimes the wife is young and beautiful, and must be borne with in spite of all; sometimes she is ugly, a shrew and a scold besides giving him horns and making him ridiculous.

The wife's complaints begin even before marriage. The husband is not of her choice, therefore everything is wrong with him. Afterwards, part of her grievance is that her husband has a devilish and unaccountable prejudice against her lover. One song, popular around the eleventh century, runs somewhat as follows: "Why does my husband beat me? Let me alone. He does not like my lover, what is the matter with him? I will give him something to worry about. . . . . I will take my lover to

140

bed with me without even a shift between us. Why does my husband beat me? Let me alone!" It has a pretty, pathetic little melody.

In Paris, near the end of the seventeenth century, a certain Gautier Garguille used to delight the daily crowds with an enormous repertory of these songs. . . . .

੨⁊

> My mother chose my husband;
> A lawyer's son was he.
> When, on the wedding night,
> He came to bed with me,
>   Ah, ah, ah! That's no way to—
>   Ah, ah, ah! That can't be!
>
> When, on the wedding night,
> He came to bed with me,
> He bit me on the shoulder
> And almost broke my knee.
>   Ah, ah, ah, etc.
>
> He bit me on the shoulder
> And almost broke my knee.
> I called my waiting-woman:
> "Come quickly, Margery!"
>
> I called my waiting-woman:
> "Come quickly, Margery,
> Go tell mama I'm dying;
> Bid her come hastily."
>
> "Go tell mama I'm dying;
> Bid her come hastily."
> Came mother to my bedside
> Before I could count three.

Came mother to my bedside
Before I could count three.
"Cheer up, my girl! What ails you
Will never kill," said she.

"Cheer up, my girl! What ails you
Will never kill," said she,
"If I had died of that, child,
God knows where *you* would be."

"If I had died of that, child,
God knows where *you* would be!
So, if you die, my daughter,
I'll grave you splendidly."

"So, if you die, my daughter,
I'll grave you splendidly,
Then carve upon your headstone
Where everyone can see—"

"Then carve upon your headstone
Where everyone can see:
'The only girl who couldn't
Survive that malady.'"

Ma Mère M'a Mariée,
Ou La Nuit de la Mariée

Ma mère m'a mariée
Au fils d'un avocat
La première nuitée
Qu'avec moi se coucha . . .

Ah, ah, ah, ça n'va guère,
Ah, ah, ah, ça n'va pas.

La première nuitée
Qu'avec moi se coucha
Il me mordit l'épaule
Et me cassa le bras.
      Ah, ah, ah, etc.

Il me mordit l'épaule
Et me cassa le bras.
J'appelai la servante:
Jeannette êtes-vous là?

J'appelai la servante:
Jeannette êtes-vous là?
Allez dire à ma mère
Que je suis au trépas.

Allez dire à ma mère
Que je suis au trépas.
Ma bonne mère arrive
Bien vite à petits pas.

Ma bonne mère arrive
Bien vite à petits pas:
"Courage! courage! ma fille
Non vous n'en mourrez pas.

Courage! courage! ma fille
Non vous n'en mourrez pas
Car si j'en étais morte
Vous ne seriez pas là.

Car si j'en étais morte
Vous ne seriez pas là
Si vous en mourrez, belle,
On vous enterrera.

Si vous en mourrez, belle,
On vous enterrera
Et puis sur votre tombe
En écrit l'on mettra: . . . . .

Et puis sur votre tombe
En écrit l'on mettra:
Ci-gît la seule en France
Qui soit morte de ça!"

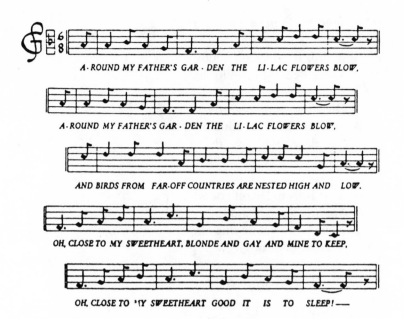

A·ROUND MY FATHER'S GAR · DEN THE LI·LAC FLOWERS BLOW,

A·ROUND MY FATHER'S GAR · DEN THE LI·LAC FLOWERS BLOW,

AND BIRDS FROM FAR·OFF COUNTRIES ARE NESTED HIGH AND LOW.

OH, CLOSE TO MY SWEETHEART, BLONDE AND GAY AND MINE TO KEEP,

OH, CLOSE TO 'IY SWEETHEART GOOD IT IS TO SLEEP! —

Oh, Close to My Sweetheart

soldiers' marching song

This song has survived for centuries and changed much in survival. It began, apparently, as a young girl's song, a spring daydream of love, and—by internal evidence—several verses were added on to make it a topical song during the invasion of the Netherlands by King Louis XIV: and the rowdy chorus is the voice of the marching soldier advertising his good fortune in love. The French troops still march to it, I am told, and there are many parodies of the verses, most of them quite unsuitable for citation in this book, or in any other for that matter.

&

Around my father's garden } *Repeat*
    The lilac flowers blow
And birds from far-off countries
    Are nested high and low.

Oh, close to my sweetheart,
Blonde and gay and mine to keep,
    Oh, close to my sweetheart
    Good it is to sleep!

And birds from far-off countries } *Repeat*
    Are nested high and low,
The quail, the gentle ring-dove,
    The pheasant bright with gold.

Oh, close to my sweetheart, etc.

The quail, the gentle ring-dove } *Repeat*
    The pheasant bright with gold,
And, day and night that singeth,
    A pigeon all my own.

And, day and night that singeth, } *Repeat*
    A pigeon all my own,
That singeth still for maidens
    Who loveless live alone.

That singeth still for maidens } *Repeat*
    Who loveless live alone:
But not for me she singeth
    For I have one to love.

But not for me she singeth } *Repeat*
    For I have one to love.
"Now, tell me, sweet-and-twenty,
    Where did your goodman go?"

"Now, tell me, sweet-and-twenty, } *Repeat*
    Where did your goodman go?"
He's gone into the Lowlands,
    The traitors have him now.

He's gone into the Lowlands, } *Repeat*
    The traitors have him now.
"What would you give, my pretty,
    To bring back your true love?"

"What would you give, my pretty, } *Repeat*
    To bring back your true love?"
I'd give the King's great palace,
    His fairest city too.

I'd give the King's great palace, } *Repeat*
    His fairest city too,
The towers of his minster,
    And the belfry of our town.

The towers of min minster, } *Repeat*
    And the belfry of our town.
And even my pretty pigeon,
    To bring back my true love.

Auprès de ma Blonde

Dans les jardins d'mon père
Les lilas sont fleuris,
Dans les jardins d'mon père
Les lilas sont fleuris,
Tous les oiseaux du monde
Vienn'nt y fair' leurs nids.

Auprès de ma blonde,
Qu'il fait bon, fait bon, fait bon,

Auprès de ma blonde,
Qu'il fait bon dormir!

Tous les oiseaux du monde
Vienn'nt y fair' leurs nids,
La caill', la tourterelle,
Et la joli' perdrix.

Après de ma blonde, etc.

La caill', la tourterelle,
Et la joli' perdrix,
Et ma joli' colombe
Qui chante jour et nuit.

Et ma joli' colombe
Qui chante jour et nuit,
Qui chante pour les filles
Qui n'ont pas fait d'ami.

Qui chante pour les filles
Qui n'ont pas fait d'ami
Pour moi ne chante guère,
Car j'en ai un joli.

Pour moi ne chante guère,
Car j'en ai un joli.
"Dites-nous donc la belle,
Ou donc est votr' ami?"

"Dites-nous donc la belle,
Ou donc est votr' ami?"
Il est dans la Hollande,
Les Hollandais l'ont pris.

Il est dans la Hollande,
      Les Hollandais l'ont pris.
Que donneriez-vous, belle,
      Pour avoir votre ami?

"Que donneriez-vous, belle,
      Pour avoir votre ami?"
Je donnerais Versailles,
      Paris et Saint-Denis.

Je donnerais Versailles,
      Paris et Saint-Denis,
Les tours de Notre-Dame
      Et l'clocher d'mon pays.

Les tours de Notre-Dame
      Et l'clocher d'mon pays,
Et me joli' colombe,
      Pour avoir mon ami.

&ar; &ar; &ar;

Song

(from the French of Clément Marot [1496–1544])
translated by Katherine Anne Porter

I am no more what once I was
And what I was no more shall be—
My jolly summer and my spring
Have taken thieves' farewell of me.

O, Love, how I have followed thee
Above all gods I thee adore—
And were I twice-born I should be
But born again to serve thee more.

translated 1933, published in
Mademoiselle, February 1943

Plus ne suis ce que j'ai été,
Et plus ne saurais jamais l'être—
Mon beau printempts et mon été
On fait le saut par la fenêtre:

Amour, tus as été mon maître,
Je t'ai servi sur tous les dieux—
Ah, si je pouvais deux fois naître
Combine je te servirais mieux!

Liberals

Life is a substance they cannot get the feel of
Goldfish or quicksilver here and yonder it slips;
Given their choice, which they haven't, they'd really rather
Go down to the boisterous sea, but not in ships.

So they go instead to live in the deep country,
But it is not in their plan to follow a plough;
They love to eat what they neither sow nor gather,
They would live simply if some one told them how.

They come back to the city where everything's cut on the bias
They point by turns with pride and view with alarm
Call for reform which they find is too much bother,
On principal they're against war, and afraid to disarm.

They would do all sorts of brave things if they dared, but they
      dare not.
It would get them in trouble with living, breathing men:
So they stay in that soft land where Wish is the father
To a liud cuckoo in a nest built by the wren. . . . .

dated 1933 by Porter, unpublished

Measures for Song and Dance

Eve gave Adam the apple;
Adam took the whole apple,
Gave Eve one bite of the apple,
And ate the rest with Lilith.

   Eve, burdened with numerous household cares,
   Abel at her breast, Cain at her knee,
   Found Adam and Lilith gorged to the ears,
   Asleep in the shade of the plundered tree.

Eve cried out upon Adam
She seized the scruff of Adam,
Asked, "Where's my apple, Adam?"
And Adam looked at Lilith.

   Lilith yawned deeply and braided her hair:
   "O, for some men of my own," said she,
   "O, for an effective leaf to wear,
   And novel fruit from a different tree!"

Eve then flew at Lilith,
She tore the braids of Lilith,
She smacked the hapless Lilith,
And Lilith screamed for Adam.

   But Adam was taken with dreadful throes;
   Holding his midriff, "Lilith!" he cried,
   "You stole Eve's apples, but never suppose
   That I can be tempted away from her side!"

The Lord gave one look at His garden,
Threw the three of them out of His garden,

Gave them a briar-patch for their garden,
And asked: "Where's that Serpent?"

In the midst of the briar-patch stood a tree
With nubbly apples of bitter flavor,
"Now this is strictly for you and me,"
Eve told Adam, "forever and ever."

Lilith cast her eyes on the young Cain,
Motioned hitherward the young Cain,
Said, "He's a likely lad, this young Cain,
And he'll find me apples."

Adam spoke to Eve: "Let's be reasonable, dear,
As an example to Cain and to Abel;
We'll have a few apples twice a year
As a special treat at the family table."

Eve frowned at Adam and Adam leered at Lilith,
Lilith smiled at Cain and Cain gazed at the tree:
His mouth watered and his eyes yearned, his stomach
   trembled:
"I like apples, too," said he.

written 1935, published in *Harper's*, 1950

Time Has Heaped a Bitter Dust

Time has heaped a bitter dust
Over her name:
Ashes are sagging on the hearth
She breathed to flame.

Her path from fire to cradle
Measured the earth:
She served the stern necessities
Of death and birth.

I take all roads and each road
Is strange to me:
I claim no kin with any wave
On any sea.

Nowhere do I stop and say
"This much is done:"
Still I fly before the winds
And the staring sun:

But this time of year her voice
On the wind's track
Follows me from her deep grave
And hails me back.

Her dust remembers its dust and calls again
back to her side this prodigal shape of her pain.

written before 1936, unpublished

Anniversary in a Country Cemetery

This time of year, this year of all years, brought
The homeless one home again;
To the fallen house and the drowsing dust
There to sit at the door,
Welcomed, homeless no more.
Her dust remembers its dust
And calls again
Back to the fallen house this restless dust
This shape of her pain.
This shape of her love
Whose living dust reposes
Beside her dust,
Sweet as the dust of roses.

written 1936; revised and published in *Harper's*, 1940;
revised 1956, 1967, 1970; published in *Collected Essays*

The Olive Grove

by R. Beltran Logroño
translated from Spanish by Katherine Anne Porter

No one quenches the olive grove
Fired with living coals.
The rains shall not quench this fire,
Nor the frost, nor the snow shall quench it.
Five boys have set ablaze this olive grove
With gasoline-soaked rags, and left to hang
Five vengeful stars among the living branches
Like silver signal lights.
O olive grove, O little olive trees!

Who now shall beat your branches for your fruit,
 Or press the oil from out your florid earth
 Burned dry by the five boys with furious hands?
Little lordlings well defended
By the guards, they burned the trees;
They are those who have wide fields, great houses,
With plentiful granaries for their ease.
They burned the trees with senseless laughter
And rattling shouts, while in the bell tower
 The priest turned the bells flying, ringing.
 O olive grove, O little olive trees!
 What man has truly beaten your branches
 Until he has fired a handful of grape shot
 through your leaves? The olive grove
 Ablaze with living flame can be quenched by no man:
 And by no rain or snow, and frost cannot quench it.
 That fire in the olive grove is spreading through all Spain.

published in . . . *and Spain Sings,* 1937

afternoon walk to her

When foot before foot and foot following faster
stirs the dust and gravel under the dropping trees
feathery pepper, thrust eucalyptus flanking me
me foot-footing, flanked by nasturtium and aster
me walking walking on my pilgrimage
there is bickering and laughter and banter
adrift on the indifferent breeze, to me on my way
confusion and crassness only a breath's blow beyond
the wood-edged way, my way today (was hardly here before)
here are alchemists at work with clay
somewhere, blinding me hastening hurrying under the tree
now a pepper now a eucalyptus now a house now
a vacant lot, songs in the air now (won't be here any more)
infusions of wonder, transforming clay
and sand of the land
and me on my way

written ca. 1946, unpublished

Morning Song of the Tinker's Bitch

When all is said that should be said
And all is done that could be done,
I've had more *fun* with men in bed—
This modest praise they've fairly won.

This modest praise they've fairly won,
When all is said that should be said,
And all is done that could be done—
I've had more fun with men in bed
    Than out of it, really.
    They're apt to be jealous in daytime,
    They act gloomy and silly.
    But I can overlook that because they *do*
    Come through
    At playtime.

                dated by Porter as 3 July 1946

After a Long Journey

(to Gene . . . . . Berlin, Fall, 1931)

This was never our season. We the spring-born, the May
children
Put on winter like a hair shirt, we dwell on death, we wait
For the turn of the year, the leap of the sun
Into the track of spring. Let us turn clasping mittened hands
Idly into the Puppen Allee of the Tiergarten.

This is not even a timely season for our love—
Kisses freeze in our mouths, our arms enfold by habit
Talking columns of stone; yet we do not talk of love,
Our love, or say again, once more, once and forever
As if it were for the first time and the last time, a long farewell
"I love you."

Once and forever words are engraved on motionless objects:
On these monuments celebrating potbellied kings, high-
    bosomed ladies,
Philosophers, comedians, tyrants, saints, slender pages
With crossed ankles and sly ambiguous smiles;
Or knights in plate armor clasping with smooth fists the hilts
Of their long-blunted answerable arguments of heroics;
Above all, on the tombs of statesmen and handsome Somebodies
    on horseback.
Besides a few poets. Stone or not, we sweat salt grief
From every pore, and our eyes continually wandering
Continually seek each other's, and we smile with a grimace like
    weeping.

Our images of travel mingle, oh, what shall we remember?

These streets of burnished iron, tender winter grass
Neatly shaven to the gray lips of water;

Hotels, cinemas—those Russian films showing Russian workingmen
Living lives of the maddest sanity, taking showers under samovar spouts,
Rossing off bottles of milk with their lunches, working like mules,
Laughing their heads off the whole time as if they were full of vodka and red pepper—

—The loud cold shudders of our ship that sailed on sea and meadow
The Caribbean, the Atlantic, the river Weser;
The spouting of whales, the bitter trap-mouthed faces of friars
In Santa Cruz de Tenerife, or the slender girls with doll hats tied to their foreheads,
And water jars on their heads running wildly sure-footed as deer
In the steep stony pathways; or the lonely music
Of the train wheels turning in the night with the lunatic tune
We never could follow?

All, all such memories are rayed metal, a star with a cutting edge,
That shears one moment from another. Must we lose them all
Or shall we do a montage of them, and frame it?

Landscapes such as the Flemish painted best are motionless
As if posing for their portraits, alive but asleep among the windmills,
Thick with the smell of warm milk-soaked hides, ruminant breathings,
Clean orderly hoofs, minute proprieties of doorways curtained with wood smoke,
Bowed under the clotted sky, bloated with winter-thick water,
Benumbed with humble certainties, snoring in a snowdrift.

If this frost stiffens our hair, we still have the taste
Of sun in our mouths, of Mexico and mangos and melons

And the feathery shade of the Peruano tree in our eyes.
The summer sea has hauled us by our shoulders down and over
    and under,
We have stretched our muscles and yawned like cats in the smell
  of cedar.

Oh, let us remember!

Catalogues of defeat, advantages, stratagems, warfares,
    successes,
Anticipations, dried glories under glass, a point of view
Petrified on its feet; medals, ribbons, citations, careers by
    appointment,
Official status propped by protocol—all these
I would leave in my will if I could to those for whom
Such things are substance, who rub these stuffs between their
    fingers for pleasure.

We will walk like ghosts of panthers in the Tiergarten:
    untamed, invisible
To the little pale eyes behind puffy lids buttoned up against the
    frail sunlight.
The swaying bellies rumble with beer. We will look at the
    garden,
Observe the dubious riches of decay, pity that fatal ripeness,
The agony of the year, the bereaved branches, the exhausted
    leaves falling
Like tears which nobody notices. O sorrow, sorrow!

Shall we ever forget how once we traveled to a far country,
A strange land, ourselves strangers to all and to each other?
The morning country of love and we two still strangers—
Our land is in winter now and the dazzle is gone from the
morning.

Ah, this was never our season, the spring-born
Wear winter like a thorn wreath, sniff the winds with cold noses

For the earliest rumor of sap, the singing thaw of rivers,
Feel under their ribs the snap of locks when the earth
Turns the key to her wine vaults and the wines flow upward.

We the May Children will be ready to drink, to unfold, to
     carouse,
We will dance on air and walk on water for joy!

Remember?

Here on a marble bench in this winter city we are presently at
     peace
To mingle the ash of our cigarettes, and to exchange our
     tokens:
A peachstone for a pigeon feather, a grasshopper wing for a sea
     shell,
A thorn from your wreath for a scrap of my hair shirt—

The spring-born in November!

published in *Mademoiselle,* 1957

Christmas Song

Sing Noël and
     Hi-de-Ho!
Sing Noël and
     Vo-de-Do!
Sing Noël both
     High! and Low!
Sing Noël and
Hey! Nonny-Nonny-No-
     ël!

written ca. 1950s, unpublished

Appendix:
Early Drafts of Poems

A. Untitled [A Dying Child]

It is quiet enough now in the house where she lay,
Watching the lattice of window vines swaying in the sun;
Saying, "oh dearly, dearly I love the light of day
And all the growing things that flower or run."

It is quiet enough now at window and on stairs,
And not again will she lift up her arms and smile and say,
"Oh dearly do I love the dress the summer garden wears,
And dearly do I love the light of day."

5 November 1920

B. Song [Now No Spring]

For my tears and my grief
Spring sends a green leaf;
For my tears and my sorrow
Summer brings a ploughed furrow.

What spring shall set me free

165

From the thing that troubles me?
What summer soothe again
With its sleepy airs and rain

The rough awakened scars of pain?

1924

C. West Indian Island

Upborne by savage dark thorns the paper lace dramatic flower
Blooming in darkness, hangs from the rock like a dancer
smiling secretly at her own image, mirrored in darkness.
    All the long day the bees cling to the oleanders,
    Pomegranates nod their heads, drowse, slowly turn
      scarlet
    At evening the tree frogs cry in the arbors
    the great hand descends, doubling itself to a hollow

    Morning comes again after what a long night, and the
      ships
    Hardly ripple the lost blue beside the coral,
    At noon a flat meadow rises in the clouds, lies serenely
    speckled with sheep and low trees and a narrow river
    hangs over the sea and smiles at its own image
the mirrored face of illusion. . . . .
    Oh, never shall I smile secretly at my own image.
Mirrored in darkness, in water, in clouds, in the faces of flowers,
It was never myself I loved, Never this solitude,
Never this landscape without figures, this darkness, this water,
This thing that sits in gaunt pride staring at water,
At ships, at pomegranates, at moons, at oleanders,
Listening to tree frogs and the flying hooves of horses, the
   sleepy whimper of birds;

166

Fearing shadows and strange sounds and the white browed cliff
 and the night,
The flash of lanterns, and the night
Which never ends, yet ends in the promise of another beginning
Blacker than the other. . . . . It was never my asking,
This pride and this fear and this solitude embodied sitting
Staring at water, at ships, at moons, at oleanders. . . . .
        Oh, Island, loosen your roots, take to the sea,
        Leap the waves like a ship, nose bravely through storms,
leave the hurricane whirling upon itself, let me return with you,
To a familiar country,
Quiet, severe, clothed in pain, full of memories,
Yet tranquil, never yet having sat staring
At unshared loveliness, at softness, at warmth, never
having listened to music of strange instruments, never having
plucked from strange air the breath of being,
will receive me as a friend, as a member
of the household, will not mock
at my solitude, my unshared thoughts, my sorrow,
my sorrow, my solitude, my unshared thought,
But will say quietly, "So, daughter, you are late,
But, come in, and welcome!"

The wind tears at the loosened shutters, slips fingers sharper
 than glass under the panes
Rips away shelter, bends the trees head to heels, loosens the feet
 of birds
        from their branches. . . . .
        So comes God straddling the whirlwind
Boasting, This is my power, but see!
I do not abuse. I am merciful
To the weak, to the sick, the hungry, the despised,
the poor in spirit!"
        Lord, what have I to do with such mercy?
        Take the roof, the floor, the wall, the ground from

under my feet.
They are yours, you made me, gave them—
Take them again, I do not claim them.
But what is mine, I keep.

So then this contest with a mythical God
goes on, this endless debate with shadows, this
colloquy between invented powers and imagined rebellions.
Now at high noon, there is calm again, with the grass flattened
under the receded flood, the broken armed trees still standing,
but wounded, but weeping, but mystified
To their hearts, but wondering,
and I say, "Brother, I wonder with you,"
To the great frogs spread belly white upon the muddy
green banks, to the birds flattened to earth, wings
spread in the miraculous gesture of flight. . . . .
to the roofless houses under the shameless sky,
the unrepentant sun, the indifferent winds. . . . .

1929

D. Bouquet for October

This is not our season, the spring-born
Put on winter like a hair shirt, remember death and wait
For the turn of the year.

It is not timely to say once for all
What love is. (Once for all words are engraved
On monuments celebrating kings, ladies,
Philosophers, clowns, slender pages with crossed ankles,
Knights clasping with smooth knuckles
Blunted answerable arguments of heroics:
Above all, on the tombs of statesmen.)

168

Streets of burnished iron, tender grass
Neatly shaven to the grey lips of water,
Hotels, cinemas, the loud cold shudders of ships,
The spouting of whales, the pocked jaws of friars, the orchestra
    of machinery,
All all such memories are rayed metal, each shears off in turn
Unless we make a sheaf of them together.

Landscapes such as the Flemish painted are justly
Asleep among windmills, thick with the smell
Of warm milk-soaked hides, ruminant breathings, clean orderly
    hoofs,
Minute proprieties of doorways curtained with wood smoke,
Shaded away from clotted sky, winter thick water,
Numbed with certainties, snoring in a snowdrift.

If the frost stiffens our hair, we have still the taste
Of sun in our teeth.
The sea has hauled us by the shoulders over and under.
We have stretched our muscles and yawned in the smell of cedar.

Catalogues of defeat, advantages, stratagems, successes, anticipa-
    tions,
Dried glories under glass, honors, a point of view petrified on its
    feet,
I would leave in my will for those to whom such things are
    substance.
We will walk in the Tiergarten: invisible
To the little eyes buttoned up against the frail sunlight:
Observe the dubious riches of decay, pity
The bereaved branches, the exhausted leaves dropping
Like tears which nobody notices.

This is not our season, the spring born
Wear winter like a thorn wreath, sniff the wind

For the earliest rumor of sap, the singing
Thaw of rivers, feel under their ribs
The snap of locks when the earth turns
The key to her wine vaults and the wines flow upwards.

Here on a marble bench we are at peace to mingle the ashes
Of our cigarettes, and to exchange our tokens:
A peach stone for a pigeon feather, a grasshopper wing for a sea
    shell.

27 September 1931

E. Anniversary in a Country Cemetery

1. [Untitled]

> This time of year, of all years, brings me
>   back
> The homeless one, home again.
> To the fallen house and the drowsing dust
> Where I sit at the door,
> Welcomed, homeless no more.
> Her dust remembers its dust and calls again
> Back to the fallen house this restless dust
> This shape of her pain.

1936

2. Birthday in a Country Cemetery

> This time of year, this year of all years
> Brought the homeless one home again:
> Back to the sunken house and the patient dust,
> There to sit at her door,
> Welcomed, homeless no more.

Her dust remembers its dust and calls again
Back to her lightless house this restless dust
This shape of her pain—

1936

3. [Untitled]

This time of year, this year of all years brought
The homeless one home again
To the fallen house and the drowsing dust
There to sit at the door
Welcomed, homeless no more.
Her dust remembers its dust and calls again
Back to the fallen house this restless dust
This shape of her pain.

"For the Journal, summer, 1936"

4. Anniversary in a Country Cemetery

This time of year, this year of all years, brought
The homeless one home again.
To the fallen house and the drowsing dust,
There to sit at the door,
Welcomed, homeless no more.
Her dust remembers its dust
And calls again
Back to the fallen house this restless dust,
This shape of her pain.

published in *Harper's Bazaar,* November 1940

5. Birthday in a Country Cemetery

This time of year, this year of all years
Brought the homeless one home again:

Back to the sunken house and the patient dust,
There to sit at her door,
Welcomed, homeless no more.
Her dust remembers its dust and calls again
Back to her lightless house this restless dust
This shape of her pain—
This shape of her love, whose living dust encloses
Her love, sweet as the dust of roses.

17 September 1956

Bibliography

Works by Katherine Anne Porter

Books

My Chinese Marriage. New York: Duffield, 1921. Reprinted as *Mae Franking's My Chinese Marriage.* Edited by Holly Franking. Austin: University of Texas Press, 1991.

Outline of Mexican Popular Arts and Crafts. Los Angeles: Young & McCallister, 1922. In *Uncollected Early Prose of Katherine Anne Porter,* 136–87.

Flowering Judas. New York: Harcourt, Brace, 1930.

Katherine Anne Porter's French Song-Book. New York: Harrison of Paris, 1933.

Flowering Judas and Other Stories. New York: Harcourt, Brace, 1935. An expansion by four stories of *Flowering Judas.*

Pale Horse, Pale Rider: Three Short Novels. New York: Harcourt, Brace, 1939.

The Days Before. New York: Harcourt, Brace, 1952.

Ship of Fools. Boston: Little, Brown, 1962.

The Collected Stories of Katherine Anne Porter. New York: Harcourt, Brace, 1965.

The Collected Essays and Occasional Writings of Katherine Anne Porter. New York: Delacorte Press, 1970.

The Never-Ending Wrong. Boston: Little, Brown, 1977. Originally published in *Atlantic* 239 (June 1977): 37–48, 53–64.

The Letters of Katherine Anne Porter. Edited by Isabel Bayley. New York: Atlantic Monthly Press, 1990.

"This Strange, Old World" and Other Book Reviews by Katherine Anne Porter. Edited by Darlene Harbour Unue. Athens: University of Georgia Press, 1991.

The Uncollected Early Prose of Katherine Anne Porter. Edited by Ruth M. Alvarez and Thomas F. Walsh. Austin: University of Texas Press, 1993.

Essays, Reviews, Short Stories

"The Shattered Star." *Everyland,* January 1920, 422–23. Reprinted in *Uncollected Early Prose.*

"The Faithful Princess." *Everyland,* February 1920, 42–43. Reprinted in *Uncollected Early Prose.*

"The Magic Ear Ring." *Everyland,* March 1920, 86–87. Reprinted in *Uncollected Early Prose.*

"The Adventures of Hadji: A Tale of a Turkish Coffee House." *Asia* 20 (August 1920): 683–84. Reprinted in *Uncollected Early Prose.*

"Striking the Lyric Note in Mexico." *New York Call,* 16 January 1921, 1, 3. (Written with Roberto Haberman.) Reprinted in *Uncollected Early Prose.*

"The New Man and the New Order." *Magazine of Mexico,* March 1921, 5–15. Reprinted in *Uncollected Early Prose.*

"Xochimilco." *Christian Science Monitor,* 31 May 1921, 10. Reprinted in *Uncollected Early Prose.*

"The Mexican Trinity." *Freeman* 3 (3 August 1921): 493–95. Reprinted, slightly revised, in *Collected Essays.*

"Where Presidents Have No Friends." *Century* 104 (July 1922): 273–84. Reprinted in *Collected Essays.*

"Two Ancient Mexican Pyramids—the Core of a City Unknown until a Few Years Ago." *Christian Science Monitor,* 19 September 1922, 7.

"María Concepción." *Century* 105 (December 1922): 224–39. Reprinted in *Collected Stories.*

"The Fiesta of Guadalupe" *El Heraldo de Mexico,* 13 December 1920, 10. reprinted in *Uncollected Early Prose* and in *Collected Essays,* where Porter dated it 1923.

"The Martyr." *Century* 106 (July 1923): 410–13. Reprinted in *Collected Stories.*

"Corridos." *Survey Graphic* 5 (May 1924): 157–59. Reprinted in *Uncollected Early Prose.*

"The Guild Spirit in Mexican Art." *Survey Graphic* 5 (May 1924): 174–78. Reprinted in *Uncollected Early Prose.*

"The Poet and Her Imp." *New York Herald Tribune,* 28 December 1924. Reprinted in *"This Strange, Old World."*

"Virgin Violeta." *Century* 109 (December 1924): 261–68. Reprinted in *Collected Stories.*

"Ay, Que Chamaco." *New Republic* 45 (23 December 1925): 141–42. Reprinted in *"This Strange, Old World."*

"A Singing Woman." *New York Herald Tribune,* 18 April 1926. Reprinted in *"This Strange, Old World."*

"He." *New Masses* 3 (October 1927): 13–15. Reprinted in *Collected Stories.*

"Magic." *transition* 13 (Summer 1928): 229–31.

"Rope." In *The Second Caravan,* edited by A. Kreymborg, 362–68. New York: McCaulay, 1928. Reprinted in *Collected Stories.*

"The Jilting of Granny Weatherall." *transition,* 15 (February 1929): 139–46. Reprinted in *Collected Stories.*

"Old Gods and New Messiahs." *New York Herald Tribune,* 19 September 1929. Reprinted in *"This Strange, Old World."*

"Theft." *Gyroscope,* November 1929, 21–25. Reprinted in *Collected Stories.*

"These Pictures Must Be Seen." *New York Herald Tribune,* 22 December 1929. Reprinted in *"This Strange, Old World."*

"Flowering Judas." *Hound and Horn* 3 (Spring 1930): 316–31. Reprinted in *Collected Stories.*

"Leaving the Petate." *New Republic* 65 (4 February 1931): 318–20. Reprinted in *Collected Essays.*

"Example to the Young." *New Republic* 66 (22 April 1931): 279–80. Reprinted in *"This Strange, Old World."*

"The Cracked Looking-Glass." *Scribner's Magazine* 91 (May 1932): 271–76, 313–20. Reprinted in *Collected Stories.*

"Hacienda." *Virginia Quarterly Review* 8 (October 1932): 556–69. Reprinted in *Collected Stories.*

"That Tree." *Virginia Quarterly Review* 10 (July 1934): 351–61. Reprinted in *Collected Stories.*

"The Grave." *Virginia Quarterly Review* 11 (April 1935): 177–83. Reprinted in *Collected Stories.*

"The Old Order." *Southern Review* 1 (Winter 1936): 495–509. (Title later changed to "The Journey," reprinted in *Collected Stories.*)

"Old Mortality." *Southern Review* 2 (Spring 1937): 686–735. Reprinted in *Collected Stories*.

"Noon Wine." *Story* 10 (June 1937): 71–103. Reprinted in *Collected Stories*.

"Pale Horse, Pale Rider." *Southern Review* 3 (Winter 1938): 417–66. Reprinted in *Collected Stories*.

"Notes on a Criticism of Thomas Hardy." *Southern Review* 6 (Summer 1940): 150–61. Reprinted as "On a Criticism of Thomas Hardy" in *Collected Essays*.

"The Leaning Tower." *Southern Review* 7 (Autumn 1941): 219–79. Reprinted in *Collected Stories*.

"A Christmas Story." *Mademoiselle* 24 (December 1946): 155, 277–79.

"Love and Hate." *Mademoiselle* 27 (October 1948): 137, 202–4, 206. Reprinted as "The Necessary Enemy" in *Collected Essays*.

"Yours, Ezra Pound." *New York Times Book Review*, 29 October 1950, 4–26. Reprinted as "'It Is Hard to Stand in the Middle'" in *Collected Essays*.

"Live Memories of a Growing Season." *Village Voice*, 29 August 1956, 4. Reprinted as "A Letter to the Editor of *The Village Voice*" in *Collected Essays*.

"The Fig Tree." *Harper's* 220 (June 1960): 55–59. Reprinted in *Collected Stories*.

"Holiday." *Atlantic Monthly* 206 (December 1960): 44–56. Reprinted in *Collected Stories*.

"On First Meeting T. S. Eliot." *Shenandoah* 12 (Spring 1961): 25–26. Reprinted in *Collected Essays*.

"From the Notebooks of Katherine Anne Porter—Yeats, Joyce, Eliot, Pound." *Southern Review*, n.s., 1 (Summer 1965): 570–73. Reprinted as "From the Notebooks: Yeats, Joyce, Eliot, Pound" in *Collected Essays*.

"Letters to a Nephew: Observations on—Pets, Poets, Sex, Love, Hate, Fame, Treason." *Mademoiselle* 62 (April 1966): 189, 244–50. Reprinted as "Letters to a Nephew" in *Collected Essays*.

Published Poems

"Texas: By the Gulf of Mexico." *Gulf Coast Citrus Fruit Grower and Southern Nurseryman* 2 (January 1912): 1.

"Enchanted." *New York Evening Post*, 25 August 1923. Reprinted in *Collected Essays*.

"Two Songs from Mexico" ("In Tepozotlan" and "Fiesta de Santiago"). *The Measure: A Journal of Poetry* 35 (January 1924): 9.

"Requiescat—." *The Measure: A Journal of Poetry* 38 (April 1924): 11. Reprinted as "Little Requiem" in *Collected Essays*.

"To a Portrait of the Poet." *Survey Graphic* 5 (May 1924): 182. A translation of a poem by Sor Juana Inés de la Cruz. Reprinted in *Uncollected Early Prose*.

"Winter Burial." *New York Herald Tribune*, 14 November 1926.

"Music of the Official Jarabe and Versos—Collected in the State of Hidalgo." *Mexican Folkways* 6, no. 1 (1930): 24. Translation of the verses of a version of the jarabe.

"Bouquet for October." *Pagany* 3 (Winter 1932): 21–22.

Katherine Anne Porter's French Song-Book. New York: Harrison of Paris, 1933. Seventeen poems translated from French.

"The Olive Grove." In . . . *and Spain Sings: Fifty Loyalist Ballads Adapted by American Poets*, edited by M. J. Benardete and Rolfe Humphries, 10. New York: Vanguard, 1937. A translation of a poem by R. Beltram Logroño.

"Anniversary in a Country Cemetery." *Harper's Bazaar*, November 1940, 139. Revised and reprinted in *Collected Essays*.

"Song (from the French of Clément Marot [1496–1544])." In "Three Poets from the South." *Mademoiselle* 16 (February 1943): 180.

"Measures for Song and Dance." *Harper's* 200 (May 1950): 80–81. Reprinted in *Collected Essays*.

"November in Windham." *Harper's* 211 (November 1955): 44. Reprinted in *Collected Essays*.

"After a Long Journey." *Mademoiselle* 46 (November 1957): 142–43. Reprinted in *Collected Essays*.

Unpublished Poems

"A Dying Child" (1920)
"Song with Castanet Accompaniment" (ca. 1921–1922)
"Variation 1001: To the Foolish Virgins Who Aren't Gathering Roses" (ca. 1922)
"Down You Mongrel, Death" (ca. 1922)
"Ordeal by Ploughshare" (1922–1923)

"This Transfusion" (1922–1923)
"Witch's Song" (1922–1923)
"Remembering Cuernavaca" (1923)
"Lights on the river" (1924)
"Now No Spring" (1924)
"First Episode" (ca. 1929)
"Morning Song" (ca. 1929)
"Night Blooming Cereus" (1929)
"West Indian Island" (1929)
"Liberals" (1933)
"Time Has Heaped a Bitter Dust" (before 1936)
"Morning Song of the Tinker's Bitch" (1946)
"afternoon walk to her" (ca. 1940s)
"Christmas Song" (ca. 1950s)

Other

Bogan, Louise. Review of *Flowering Judas,* by Katherine Anne Porter. *New Republic* 64 (22 October 1930): 277–78.

Boyd, Nancy [Edna St. Vincent Millay]. *Distressing Dialogues.* New York: Harper and Brothers, 1924.

Brenner, Anita. *Idols behind Altars.* New York: Payson and Clarke, 1929.

Burke, Kenneth. "Four Master Tropes." *A Grammar of Motives.* Berkeley: University of California Press, 1969.

Chamberlain, John. "Books of the Times." Review of *Flowering Judas and Other Stories,* by Katherine Anne Porter. *New York Times,* 11 October 1935, L-23.

Child, Francis, ed. *The English and Scottish Popular Ballads.* 5 vols. Boston: Houghton Mifflin, 1882–1898.

Covarrubias, Miguel. *The Prince of Wales and Other Famous Americans: Caricatures by Miguel Covarrubias.* New York: Alfred A. Knopf, 1925.

De la Selva, Salomón. *Tropical Town and Other Poems.* New York: John Lane Company, 1918.

DeMouy, Jane. *Katherine Anne Porter's Women: The Eye of Her Fiction.* Austin: University of Texas Press, 1983.

Eliot, T. S. *From Poe to Valéry*. New York: Harcourt, Brace, 1948.
———. *Poems*. London: Hogarth Press, 1919.
Freud, Sigmund. *A General Introduction to Psychoanalysis*. Translated by Joan Riviere. Garden City, N.Y.: Garden City Publishing, 1920.
Gannett, Lewis. "Books and Things." Review of *Pale Horse, Pale Rider: Three Short Novels*, by Katherine Anne Porter. *New York Herald Tribune*, 30 March 1939.
Givner, Joan. *Katherine Anne Porter: A Life*. New York: Simon and Schuster, 1982. Athens: University of Georgia Press, 1992 (2d ed., revised).
———, ed. *Katherine Anne Porter: Conversations*. Jackson: University of Mississippi Press, 1987.
Hartley, Lodwick. "Katherine Anne Porter." *Sewanee Review* 48 (April–June 1940): 206–16.
Hilt, Kathryn, and Ruth M. Alvarez. *Katherine Anne Porter: An Annotated Bibliography*. New York: Garland, 1990.
Housman, A. E. *The Collected Poems*. New York: Holt, Rinehart and Winston, 1965.
Lopez, Enrique Hank. *Conversations with Katherine Anne Porter: Refugee from Indian Creek*. Boston: Little, Brown, 1981.
McGuire, William. *Poetry's Catbird Seat: The Consultantship in Poetry in the English Language at the Library of Congress, 1937–1987*. Washington: Library of Congress, 1988.
Millay, Edna St. Vincent. *Collected Poems*. New York: Harper and Brothers, 1956.
Mooney, Harry John, Jr. *The Fiction and Criticism of Katherine Anne Porter*. Pittsburgh: University of Pittsburgh Press, 1957.
Nervo, Amado. *Obras Completas*. 2 vols. Madrid: Aguilar, 1962.
Recent Southern Fiction: A Panel Discussion. Macon, Ga.: Wesleyan College, 1961.
Percy, Bishop. *Reliques of Ancient English Poetry: consisting of old heroic ballads, songs and other pieces of our earlier poets, . . . together with some few of later date*. London: J. Dodsley, 1765.
"Poetry of Our Times." *Variety*, 29 April 1953, 39.
Pound, Ezra. *Cathay*. London: Elkin Mathews, 1915.
———. *The Letters of Ezra Pound: 1907–1941*. Edited by D. D. Paige. New York: Harcourt, Brace, 1950.
———. *Pavannes and Divisions*. New York: Alfred A. Knopf, 1918.

Rosenfeld, Paul. "An Artist in Fiction." *Saturday Review of Literature* 19 (1 April 1939): 7.

Schwartz, Edward G. "The Fictions of Memory." *Southwest Review* 45 (Summer 1960): 204–15.

Tate, Allen. *Mr. Pope and Other Poems.* Freeport, N.Y.: Books for Libraries Press, 1928.

Thompson, Barbara. "Katherine Anne Porter: An Interview." *Paris Review* 8 (Winter–Spring 1963): 87–114. Reprinted in Givner, *Conversations.*

Trueblood, Alan S. *A Sor Juana Anthology.* Cambridge: Harvard University Press, 1988.

Walsh, Thomas F. *Katherine Anne Porter and Mexico: The Illusion of Eden.* Austin: University of Texas Press, 1992.

Warren, Robert Penn. "Irony with a Center: Katherine Anne Porter." *Kenyon Review* 4 (Winter 1942): 29–42.

———. *Promises: Poems 1954–1956.* New York: Random House, 1957.

Wescott, Glenway. "Katherine Anne Porter Personally." In *Images of Truth,* 25–58. New York: Harper and Row, 1962.

Winters, Yvor. "Major Fiction." *Hound and Horn* 4 (January–March 1931): 303–5.

Wylie, Elinor. *Collected Poems.* New York: Alfred A. Knopf, 1954.

Index